PRAISE FOR
THE WOMAN'S BOOK
OF MINDFULNESS

"The Woman's Book of Mindfulness is a warmhearted tour of many effective ways for a woman to feel more peaceful, focused, and happy in the middle of her busy life. Based on scientific research and its author's deep insights, it is comprehensive and caring…a wonderful book."

—Rick Hanson, PhD, psychologist and author of Buddha's Brain, Resilient, Hardwiring Happiness, and Neurodharma

"All of the women in my life will be receiving a copy of The Woman's Book of Mindfulness. I am a forty-year veteran of meditation, and I've taught mindfulness professionally for many years. However, mindfulness is an ever-evolving practice and there's always more to learn. I gained so much from Sue Patton Thoele's insight. This book is full of soulful information, delivered in the kindest, gentlest, and most supportive way. It's a must-read for women of all ages."

—Kim Colegrove, author of Mindfulness for Warriors and creator of Pause First Academy

"Sue Thoele is the master of explicating real life and real people. In The Woman's Book of Mindfulness, she adds a new dimension: real thinking. Many books preach mindfulness, but this is the only one that makes it so simple that you fall into practicing it as you turn the pages. Thoele has surpassed even her early groundbreaking books tailored to women's needs.

Here is the hallmark of a deeply intuitive writer who presents her message in gentle, nonjudgmental, and attractively intimate prose."

—Hugh Prather, author of Morning Notes, Notes to Myself, and Spiritual Notes to Myself

"Sue Patton Thoele is a heart-filled and gifted wordsmith who draws you into an enchanted journey of personal growth in each of her books. The Woman's Book of Mindfulness may well be her crowning glory—and yours—so get ready for a big treat!"

—Bobbie Sandoz Merrill, MSW, author of Settle for More, Parachutes for Parents, In the Presence of High Beings, and Compelling Conversations with Dolphins and Whales in the Wild

"A wise, witty, and wonderful guide to what eludes us most: peace of mind and heart in a turbulent world."

—Janice Lynne Lundy, DMin, author of Your Truest Self, My Deepest Me, Portable Peace, and Thank You is My Prayer

"The Woman's Book of Mindfulness is a joyful reminder of our inherent capacity to meet the challenges of life with loving awareness. This delightful book invites us to soften into the wisdom of our own heart with kindness, acceptance, and mindfulness. Learning alongside Sue as she deepens into her own practices feels like reconnecting with a dear friend who embodies her wholeness and power. Full of compassionate guidance, clear processes, and engaging stories, this book is perfect for women who are starting their mindfulness practice and those who are already familiar with these essential ways of being."

—Harmony Kwiker, MA, author of Reveal: Embody the True Self Beyond Trauma and Conditioning, psychotherapist, and adjunct professor at Naropa University

"What I love most about Sue Patton Thoele's book is that I'm awash in calm simply from reading it! Her loving language is like a warm bath with eucalyptus bubbles when I'm weary. I bask in her kind, inviting language: 'savor, accept, enjoy, bless, open.' Thoele offers novel ways to practice mindfulness that go way beyond our usual ideas of meditation or breathing exercises. She helps us look in new directions to explore gentle and compassionate pathways to quiet our minds and experience more awareness. This book is a sigh of relief, it is a deep breath of cool mountain air, it is a squeeze of lime in sparkling mineral water. This book? It feels like 'ahhhh.' Thank you, Sue Thoele, for giving us overwhelmed and overextended folks a much-needed break."

—Sherry Richert Belul, author of Say It Now: 33 Creative Ways to Say I Love You to the Most Important People in Your Life

"When there is so much to deal with these days, it may seem impossible to live mindfully. But that is what I love about this book. With simple yet powerful ideas, The Woman's Book of Mindfulness shows you that being mindful is not only possible, but essential for a happier, healthier, and more joyous life."

—Allen Klein, author of The Awe Factor

"In The Woman's Book of Mindfulness: Gentle Practices for Restoring Calm, Finding Hope, and Opening Your Heart, Sue Thoele provides a clear and easily practiced roadmap for greater peace and happiness in this time of great uncertainty and upheaval in the world. Sue's wisdom and experience in practicing mindfulness in her life demonstrates that at every moment we have the choice to wake up to the present moment. Thank you, Sue, for this powerful invitation to greater calm, hope, and love in our daily lives."

—Susyn Reeve, author of Heart Healing: The Power of Forgiveness to Heal a Broken Heart

"Sue Thoele's The Woman's Book of Mindfulness is exactly what our hearts (and minds) need now. Part mindfulness guidebook, part positivity manual, Thoele's gracious work moves beyond the buzzword to offer practical healing methods and real-life examples. She asks us to be gentle with ourselves, and in doing so, gifts us her experience as a roadmap. Do yourself a favor and pick up two gift copies—the first a gift for yourself, and the second a gift for a woman you adore."

—Nita Sweeney, award-winning author of Depression Hates A Moving Target and You Should Be Writing

THE
Woman's
Book of
Mindfulness

OTHER BOOKS BY SUE

Strength: Meditations for Wisdom, Balance & Power

The Courage to Be Yourself

The Woman's Book of Courage

Autumn of the Spring Chicken

Heart Centered Marriage

The Woman's Book of Confidence

Freedoms After 50

The Woman's Book of Spirit

Excellent as You Are

Growing Hope

The Courage to Be a Stepmom

The Woman's Book of Soul

The Courage to Be Yourself Journal

THE

Woman's Book of Mindfulness

Finding Freedom Through
Awareness, Acceptance,
and Self-Compassion

SUE PATTON THOELE

Books That Save Lives

Cover Design: Megan Werner
Cover Photo: YALÇIN KAHYA / stock.adobe.com
Interior Design & Layout: Jermaine Lau
Author Photo: Brett Hall

Published by BTSL/Jim Dandy Publishing

For special orders, quantity sales, course adoptions and corporate sales, please email the publisher at info@jimdandypublishing.com. For trade and wholesale sales, please contact Ingram Publisher Services at customer.service@ingramcontent.com or +1.800.509.4887.

The Woman's Book of Mindfulness: Finding Freedom Through Awareness, Acceptance, and Self-Compassion

Library of Congress Cataloging-in-Publication number: 2024947277
ISBN: (p) 978-1-68481-719-1 (e) 978-1-68481-720-7
BISAC category code SEL021000, SELF-HELP / Motivational & Inspirational

To the myriad kind and courageous caretakers of humans,
critters, and the environment.

Thank you!

Table of Contents

Chapter 3

Chapter 4

Chapter 5

Chapter 9

Part III
Enjoying the Benefits

Chapter 10

Do You Know What Your Mind Is Doing?

I'm honored to be writing the foreword to Sue Patton

Thoele's The Woman's Book of Mindfulness for two reasons. The first is because in my work helping CEOs and other executives around the world grow and change, something she taught me decades ago is one of the things I most often say to my clients: Be gentle with yourself and others. It was the self part I needed to learn most about.

Sue taught me self-compassion long before it had a name and researchers and institutes. It's such an important lesson. We can't truly change if we aren't kind to ourselves. Harshness creates shame, and shame is a toxic emotion that we draw away from. We run mentally from whatever is causing that feeling, and thus we don't learn and grow. Plus shaming ourselves causes adrenaline and cortisol to go racing through our systems, and we all have too much of that already! Gentleness or self-compassion produces oxytocin, the love hormone, which makes us feel calmer, more capable, and therefore better able to transform.

Sue's gentle approach runs through every thought and word in this book. She treats you kindly as a reader and hopefully that will translate to how you treat yourself as you explore being more mindful in your life.

Which brings me to the second reason I am grateful to be introducing this book to you: there is nothing more important right now in the world than the cultivation of mindfulness. It's not the only thing we have to do to heal our world and find our way together. But it is the base from which we create wise thought, wise speech, and wise action.

Here's why: Mindfulness creates what interpersonal neurobiologist Dr. Daniel Siegel calls mindsight, the ability of the mind to observe the mind. Mindsight "helps us get ourselves off of the autopilot of ingrained behaviors and habitual responses," writes Siegel on his mindsight website, which gives us greater options of response: Oh, I see I am about to say something unkind; do I really want to do that? That noticing, that awareness, is where transformation is born. The more we know what our minds are doing, the more we become in charge of them, then we can respond more, rather than react.

And it's not just our thinking that gets better, but our emotional responses as well. With mindsight, we are able to "name and tame" the emotions we are experiencing, rather than being overwhelmed by them. Labeling creates a space between ourselves and our feelings that allows us to dig fewer holes that are hard to get out of.

Mindsight has been called many other names: "Going to the balcony," the Witness Self, your wise mind. Whatever you call it, it's the part of your mind that knows what your mind is doing. And growing that capacity is the door not only to freedom, but to truly being able to "live gently with yourself and others." May this journey bring you greater kindness, peace, and connection.

—MJ Ryan

Introduction

An Ongoing Quest

I am thankful for the opportunity to republish The Woman's Book of Mindfulness during this incredibly intense and life-changing time. As the world reels from the effects of a pandemic and the United States is being called to live up to its name by ending racism and inequality, the opportunity to explore what many of us yearn for in our heart of hearts is an honor. Even in the best of times, women want peace of mind, open hearts, and an enduring sense of balance and purpose. We want to dispel fear with steadfast gratitude, compassion, and hope. And especially in uncertain times filled with anguish and outrage, we need to love ourselves as deeply and unselfishly as we do others. We want to make a positive difference, be heard, and feel fulfilled.

Can learning to live mindfully grant us these desires? I don't know, but I do know I feel more openhearted, calm, and hopeful since discovering the promise and practice of mindfulness. Although I'm sure age and circumstances are factors in my softening toward myself and life in general, I'm continually amazed by the calm joy that so often accompanies mindfulness...when I remember to do it.

While I'm not an expert on mindfulness, I am passionately committed to increasing mindfulness and presence in both my inner and outer journeys. I leaped at the chance to write about mindfulness because one of the best ways to learn something at a deep and enduring level is to study and teach it. However, in the process of trying to practice what I write, I'm alternately appalled and amused by just how elusive mindfulness can be—and how incredibly easy it is for me to be seduced away from simplicity and focused awareness into multitasking and rampant mind-mucking.

The other day I caught myself being absentminded as I was simultaneously bringing up my emails, scrubbing allergy-inducing cat dander off my computer screen, and obsessing about the state of the not-so-unified union. There was no harm done in that episode of mindlessness, and I even felt a little amused when I became conscious of it. However, when I'm too exhausted to sleep because I'm overcommitted, obsessively fretting about people or circumstances I can't change, resentful, or chastising myself for something, that's not funny. How I wish I'd known about mindfulness and conscious presence when I was a single mom losing sleep over many nights, worrying about how I was going to take care of myself and my sons.

Thankfully, both science and psychology now recognize that the stress of busy mindlessness is epidemic in our society. Many of us know from experience that unrelenting, helter-skelter thoughts and behaviors can result in damaged health, poor relationships, and a chaotic mind, to name only a few harmful effects. We can alter stress-provoking behavior. Awareness is the first step in making positive change. Knowing that mindlessness increases stress, we can choose to turn toward mindfulness, which roots us deeply in the moment and plants us firmly in the reality of now. Even when now is painful and difficult, mindfulness can help neutralize inner and outer chaos and invite balance and harmony into our lives and beings.

Searching for the grace that comes with mindful living is an ongoing quest. When grace holds my hand during comfortable times, I feel in-the-flow with all that is good and right within and around me and life seems joyous, light, fun, and comforting. During challenging yet mindful times, life can feel rich, fertile, and growth producing. So why are mindful times inconsistent? Why do I too often feel the need to exhort myself to "Slow down! Shut up! Stay open!" in a manner that contradicts my long-term motto of Live gently with yourself and others?

I imagine mindful times are rarer than I would like because my energy is jangled and scattered, my awareness snagged on the past or the future—a fragment weighing problematic options, a slice gnawing on the malfunctioning computer, a wedge worried about injustice or a struggling adult child. In other words, when I'm not inhabiting my life right now, there's no place for balance, harmony, and hope to stick. Now is the only time anything truly exists. Right now—this moment, this experience, this feeling, this interaction—is your life. All else is shadow and smoke, often colored by fear.

Consciously living in the moment is at the core of mindfulness practices. To be mindful is to be truly alive. Mindfulness allows you to be fully present to your authentic self and to live your life with acute awareness and an open heart. Does this mean you may experience pain more deeply? Possibly. Will mindfulness bring you more joy and serenity? Yes, I've found that to be true. Is it worth the effort? For me, absolutely. Because you are reading this, my bet is you already have tasted the depth, meaning, and magic of mindful living and would love to experience more of it.

My intention for The Woman's Book of Mindfulness is that it defines mindfulness in an easily understood way, provides stories and examples of women who find mindful living rewarding, and gives you many practices that can make the path easier and more fun should you choose to pursue it. My wish for The Woman's Book of Mindfulness is that it provides a springboard for both you and me from which we can dive openheartedly into the numinous now and live our lives more fully, joyously, and consciously. I hope the stories included in the book not only inspire you but also allow you to feel you have friends along the way. They show that I—and all the women portrayed in these pages—lurch, stumble, fall, and forget a thousand times, but the beautiful feelings of peace, joy, relaxation, and openheartedness that mindfulness brings keep us recommitting to the journey.

The Woman's Book of Mindfulness can be used in a variety of ways— as a meditation guide, a daily friend and reminder, or the answer to a specific question. If you want to make one particular practice a habit, try concentrating on it for twenty-one days straight. Experts have found it takes twenty-one days to either break an old habit or create a new one. You can also ask for the perfect, right entry for the moment and open the book at random. Random opening is intuitive and fun and sometimes elicits an amazed "No way!" Or you may enjoy the process of moving through the book in sequence. Trust yourself and use The Woman's Book of Mindfulness in ways that speak to your heart in the moment. There is no right or wrong way to practice.

Although the myriad practices within these pages have helped other women create minutes of mindfulness and oases of awareness amid the hustle, hassle, and grief of everyday life, they are by no means the be-all and end-all. You probably either already know of exercises and practices specifically tailored to your desires and needs, or you will be drawn to create them.

Each of us has the ability to nurture mindfulness in her own unique way. The peace of mind and heart gained from a mindful attitude is well worth the commitment. Mindfulness helps us love ourselves more gently and completely. Wrapped in the comfort and security of self-love, our hearts naturally open and love flows more freely to others. And love is the essence of all that matters.

PART I

Exploring the Basics

Chapter 1

What Is Mindfulness and Why Do We Want It?

"Mindfulness means paying attention in a particular way: on purpose, in the present moment, and nonjudgmentally."

—Jon Kabat-Zinn

Mindfulness is being aware of yourself, others, and your surroundings in the moment. When consciously and kindly focusing awareness on life as it unfolds minute by precious minute, you are better able to savor each experience. Also, being closely attentive gives you the opportunity to change unwise or painful feelings and responses quickly. In fact, being truly present in a mindful way is an excellent stress reducer; because of that, it can be seen as consciousness conditioning, a strengthening workout for body, mind, heart, and spirit.

While few of us have the temperament, financial freedom, or life circumstances that allow long periods of meditation, extended retreats, or endless Zen walks, we can gather scattered energy and awareness by practicing mindful moments each and every day! In time, moments become minutes, and minutes ultimately become a more present and peaceful way of life.

ELEMENTS OF MINDFULNESS

To make mindfulness more accessible, I've highlighted four elements I believe are essential in day-to-day practice. They are paying attention, inhabiting the moment, simplifying, and breath. There are, of course, numerous facets to each element of mindfulness, and we will explore many of them in Part II, "The Practices."

The Four Elements of Mindfulness:

- ☒ Paying Attention
- ☒ Inhabiting the Moment
- ☒ Simplifying
- ☒ Breathing

Paying Attention

When you focus your awareness on someone or something, you are paying attention. You have narrowed your field of vision and chosen to look at the person or thing through mental and emotional binoculars. The object of your attention becomes your focal point. Focused attention allows you to see clearly and in finer detail. Interestingly, almost any person (or thing) to whom we pay close attention gains value in our hearts and minds. Concentrated awareness leads to better understanding and appreciation of that to which we are attentive to. For instance, truly listening to someone and hearing them at a meaningful level adds richness and depth to the relationship. By compassionately focusing your attention on another, it's possible to understand their thoughts, feelings, desires, and doubts more intimately. Deep understanding opens your heart. While the unknown can feel threatening or suspicious, the known is more easily lovable. Very often, to know and understand another is to love them.

Attention is an invaluable gift to give.

During a discussion of mindfulness with my son Brett, he said, "I think the reason I love adrenaline-rush sports so much is that I have to stay present and pay attention. Because if I don't, it could be a matter of life or death." Just what a mother wants to hear, right? He does have a great point, however. While not paying attention to yourself may not catapult you off a mountain cornice to your doom or grind you into the sand beneath a monstrous wave as it could my son, neglecting yourself over time is so wearing that you can lose your joy and enthusiasm for life. Lack of attention may not physically kill you but having heard myself and many other women say, "This is killing me!" and "I feel empty and dead inside," and "I think this relationship/job/stress is sucking the life right out of me." I know that self-neglect is very harmful indeed.

Because paying loving attention often results in valuing, understanding, and enjoying what you pay attention to, it's incredibly important you place yourself at—or very near—the top of your pay-attention-to list! Just as knowing and understanding another often leads to loving them more fully, the same is true with yourself. Gently and lovingly paying attention to yourself offers you the opportunity to know, understand, and accept yourself more completely, and consequently, it can allow you to fall in love with yourself just the way you are in this moment.

Another bonus received from paying close attention to ourselves and the moment at hand is that we recognize habits and behaviors that no longer add value and joy to our lives. Being conscious of counterproductive or self-sabotaging actions, reactions, and responses as they happen gives you the opportunity to stop and make a different choice, one that is more conducive to health and peace of mind. Focusing awareness on the now not only gives you the opportunity to change what isn't working, it also allows you to enhance and appreciate what is working. Out of habit or fear, when feeling pressured or rushed, it's easy to randomly circle the drain and cling to what is driving us crazy. Thankfully, mindful living leads to an intentional life that is purposeful and promotes calm, balance, and peace of mind and heart.

Inhabiting the Moment

As a psychotherapist who believes much of our healing comes from understanding and forgiving the past, and as someone who loves to revisit wonderful experiences in order to revel in the feelings they elicited the first time around, I've struggled with the concept of continually living in the moment. What does living in the moment really mean? Where does planning for the future, scheduling appointments in advance, and making reservations for a future trip fit into the idea of living in the moment? How can living moment to moment complement my forays into the past and my need to stay sane by preparing for things to come?

Once when I was talking to my chosen daughter, Colleen, about not having come to a satisfactory conclusion about living in the moment, she said, "I've been thinking about that too, and I've decided that what I am consciously doing in the moment is the moment." Aha! The proverbial light bulb went on, and then living in the moment became a believable and doable objective. For me, consciously is the significant word here. As I understand it, when we consciously do, think, or experience something, our attention is fully engaged and we are connected with the reality and texture of what is going on. Therefore, if we are consciously paying attention and aware of planning for the future or thinking of the past right here, right now, we are still inhabiting the moment.

While I believe mindfulness can include understanding and savoring the past and/or planning, imagining, and envisioning the future, we will concentrate on the description given by renowned long-term teachers who see mindfulness as being consciously, compassionately, and nonjudgmentally present to what is happening now. It's important to focus on staying in the moment, because although we can remain mindful of the here and now when we consciously project our thoughts into the future or decide to move back in time to review the past, it is incredibly easy to fall out of a mindful state when our thoughts switch to automatic and skitter off in many directions.

Contrary to how it may sound, mindfulness is not arduous or overwhelming. In reality, mindfulness is calming, grounding, and centering. Nonetheless, I can still almost hear you gasping, as my friend Cynthia once did, "What! How can I—multitasking wizard, perfectionist, codependent, always with an ear, eye, or hand distracted toward other people's needs— become a mindful woman?" The answer is simple although not necessarily easy. We become mindful women through intentional practice, practice, practice.

I'm sure you've heard the saying, "Take it one day at a time." While a day at a time is a great concept, a full day may contain way too much for us to handle during certain circumstances like intense grief, physical pain, or fear. In soul-searing situations, taking it one minute or one breath at a time may be the most we can do. The same small-step principle works in your practices for becoming a more mindful woman. Take it one tiny, easygoing little step at a time. At least that's how I, and other women I know, are progressing toward increased mindfulness: one gentle, conscious moment at a time. In fact, the theme of The Woman's Book of Mindfulness is that a few mindful moments can make a world of difference.

Simplifying

Even though therapists and spiritual teachers, including the Dalai Lama, assure us that simplifying our lives will make us happier, not only do many of us have plates full to overflowing, but we are also juggling several plates at once. As a result, our time and energy can become fragmented by trying to answer the braying demands of multiple obligations and opportunities. Because we are many things to many people, it's easy to be on-call twenty-four seven to everyone else and forget ourselves. One of my clients explained her experience of obligation-overwhelm as feeling "nibbled to death by ducks."

Gently coaxing yourself back into the now by moving your attention away from the army of ducks seemingly poised for future attack and choosing to focus only on the ducks nibbling in the moment helps alleviate feelings of overwhelm. You can usually manage almost anything if you simplify by taking it one small step at a time, one little bite at a time…moment by moment. I've found that making detailed lists is also a great help in implementing the small-step approach to almost anything. Of course, there are extraordinary times of exhaustion, illness, stress and grief when the moment itself is so overwhelming that no amount of simplification helps. In those dire times, we need to allow others to help us.

But even in extreme situations, and definitely in day-to-day reality, mindful living helps us opt for the serenity of simplicity—the blessing of feeling underwhelmed—and gives us the ability to recognize whatever comfort is available in the moment. Because mindful minutes calm our souls, quiet our minds, and open our hearts, they are well worth the effort of learning and incorporating into our lives.

There are countless ways to simplify your inner and outer lives, and most of them bring at least a modicum of relief and relaxation. My friend Sophie, who recently retired, is now happily simplifying her home by throwing out at least twenty-seven things a day and organizing to her heart's content. Her heart is actually more content. "All the clutter was affecting me physically and emotionally," she said enthusiastically, "I'm already feeling so much lighter and freer and proud of myself." With the luxury of time, Sophie is bringing more balance and harmony into her home and heart by getting rid of material things that are no longer necessary or helpful.

In the process of simplifying her physical space, Sophie is clearing and cleansing interior space as well. You may benefit from doing the same. If you have a habit of castigating yourself with derogatory self-talk like "You dummy, you!" it needs to be thrown out. Or perhaps you are lugging around an old grudge or injury that needs to be forgiven in order for love to flow freely from and to you. How much simpler our lives are when we toss such things in the trash and symbolically burn them into transformation.

Simple is calming. Simple is satisfying.

Simplifying creates inner and outer space: space invites serenity.

Breathing

Breath is the bridge between body and mind and it's the gateway to the present moment. By focusing on your breath, you can easily bring yourself into the here and now and attune mind and heart to your physical body. Many of the practices in Part II focus on ways you can use breath to increase mindfulness and body awareness. Breath practices are centered around the following guidelines:

☒   Bringing attention to breath

☒ Deepening breath

☒ Directing breath

Breathing is the first thing we do after birth and the last thing we do before death. Breath is life. Breath is a master teacher. Using your breath consciously and constructively enhances your vitality, increases daily joy, opens you more fully to love, and brings you richly and deeply into the practice of mindfulness.

MYTHS OF MINDFULNESS

Having just explained how I view mindfulness and outlined the four elements we will be concentrating on in The Woman's Book of Mindfulness, I'd now like to highlight a couple of myths about mindfulness.

Myth 1. Mindfulness Is Meditation

Although mindfulness and meditation do bring similar benefits and are both intended to quiet and center body, mind, and spirit, meditation is something we do, while mindful is something we are. Meditation is an intentional oasis in which you renew and replenish yourself. In meditation, you quiet your mind, body, and spirit in order to reconnect with yourself and your Source. Meditation is an activity. Mindfulness is an intentional adjustment of attitude and focus: a way of being.

Meditation supports and encourages mindfulness by training our wandering minds to be quietly aware and deliberately present. Because of its complementary nature, many of the practices included in The Woman's Book of Mindfulness are meditations. We do them to calm, center, and quiet ourselves and to diminish the tendency to become lost in thought. Such meditations strengthen the mindful muscles needed to develop the habit of mindful awareness.

Myth 2. Mindfulness Is Difficult and Time-Consuming

Because mindfulness is an attitude and way of being, we can move into it as easily and quickly as changing channels on the television. The only difficult parts of mindfulness are remembering to practice it, and to not judge ourselves when we forget, but simply and kindly choose to move back into the moment and pay attention to what is going on.

Mindfulness actually saves time and energy because it eliminates the wear and tear that being sucked unconsciously into the past or future causes our psyches, souls, and selves. Although we can heal the past and plan for the future, we cannot change or control either, which often makes dwelling on them an exercise in frustration and impotence. Mindfulness is also helpful for keeping track of mundane yet crucial details, like where you put your car keys and the time of your next appointment.

DIFFERENCES BETWEEN MINDFUL AND AUTOMATIC LIVING

All of us shift into automatic pilot occasionally. I know I do. But I didn't know how much I did until I decided it would be fun to take an inventory of my own mindful vs. automatic living quotient. During one particular day, I curiously jotted down the times I noticed either mindful or mechanical actions or conversations. I was definitely wrong about the exercise being fun! Noticing how often I did or said things by rote—while knowing that I probably missed about a million mindless examples—brought me up short and helped cement my commitment to living more mindfully one little step at a time. As a result of my experiment, I realized that automatic living is essentially the opposite of mindfulness.

Because of the demands on our time and attention, many of us shift into overdrive in the morning and speed through the hours simply trying to get everything done that is expected of us or we expect of ourselves. At the end of such a day, it's easy to wonder where the hours went, what we accomplished during them, and more importantly, whether we feel it was a day wasted or well spent.

Sometimes just listing a few of the differences between mindful and automatic living gives us a clearer realization of the Mindful/Automatic ratio in our own daily lives. The following examples barely scratch the surface of the differences between mindfulness and un-awakened automation, but I imagine you can fill in the blanks with your own personal favorites.

Mindful Living is	Automatic Living is
Conscious	Unconscious
Creative	Habitual
Calm	Restless
Simple	Complex
Purposeful	Chaotic
Responsible	Blaming
Mature	Immature
Grateful	Complaining
Empowered	Controlling
Openhearted	Fearful, protective
Relaxed	Rushed
Focused	Scattered
Whole	Fragmented

The antithesis of mindfulness is apparent in driving. My son once referred to driving as "down time," but given the number of accidents and injuries happening every day, that's probably not the best way to approach it. Many of us use driving time to multitask and divide our time between the road, the phone, lunch, scolding kids, and mind-wandering. Police officers are now routinely asking drivers if they were on their cell phones at the time of an accident or infraction. Just the other day, I realized my inner autopilot had driven a few miles without me being aware of the road at all. Ironically, I was thinking about the topic of mindfulness so diligently at the time that I became my own bad example.

Mindful living promotes peace and awareness, while a mind automatically overflowing with a million attention-grabbing thoughts and worries often creates anxiety, depression, and disappointment. When we're stretched to the limit and distracted by inner and outer demands, it's impossible to see anything clearly. Given the superhuman pace at which we often run, is it any wonder life seems to pass in a blur? On the other hand, mindfully moving through our days can bring a great sense of calm, balance, and joy. Even though I'm forever failing to remain mindful, simply holding an intention toward mindfulness and continuing to practice, practice, practice makes me feel good. Sir Winston Churchill's statement "Success consists of going from failure to failure without loss of enthusiasm" seems appropriate for the practice of mindfulness. We will fail to be mindful each moment—everyone does. But we can remain enthusiastic and glean benefits from our practice no matter how perfect or imperfect it is.

A WORD ABOUT WOMEN

Even though the practice of mindfulness is deeply rooted in ancient, monastic traditions, I believe women are uniquely suited to its practice because we are naturally blessed with qualities such as sensitivity and diffuse awareness. Diffuse awareness is the ability to comfortably perceive and understand many things at once. Sensitivity is having feelings about what is seen, understood, and experienced. Women are multifaceted, multitasking wonders. We are aware of and can pay attention to multiple things at once while also noting how we are feeling within the process. These are natural talents conducive to mindful living.

The upside of sensitivity and diffuse awareness is that nothing much slips by us; the downside is exactly the same thing. Nothing much slips by us. Although being acutely aware of and responsive to both subtle nuances and obvious occurrences is helpful in many areas of life—both childrearing and career-building spring to mind—such heightened sensitivity can also be overwhelming.

Sensitivity, Awareness, and Me

"I carry the weight of the world on my shoulders and feel overwhelmed and exhausted." a client lamented. I certainly could identify with her since I, too, felt overwhelmed for many years and made it worse by chastising myself for being a bad mom, wife, therapist, or whatever other hat I was wearing at the time. Yes, raising four kids, learning to live with two husbands—spectacularly unsuccessfully with one—running a household, cooking, and creating two careers, as well as doing the everyday necessities can be very exhausting. But I exacerbated the difficult feelings by neither understanding nor taking care of myself as well as I could have.

Noticing how often I felt overwhelmed, a friend recommended I read Elaine Aron's The Highly Sensitive Person: How to Survive When the World Overwhelms You. In the preface, the author states, "Having a sensitive nervous system is normal, a basically neutral trait. You probably inherited it. It occurs in about 15 to 20 percent of the population." (xiii) Professor Aron goes on to explain that highly sensitive people's nervous systems are physically wired in ways that cause them to become overaroused and overstimulated more easily than most people.

Taking the self-test in the book showed beyond a shadow of a doubt, I was a highly sensitive person, an HSP. What an incredible relief to be labeled "normal" and to begin to let go of the gnawing fear that I was fundamentally defective or emotionally flawed beyond repair. Understanding that nervous system wiring—a physiological phenomenon—made me a sensitive person, not a weak wimp, or worse, a teeth-grinding bitch, continues to be an incredibly freeing insight.

Sound is the area of my greatest sensitivity. At the time I learned I was highly sensitive, my household was comprised of one husband, four teenagers, three dogs, a cat, and multiple friends-of-teenagers. As you can imagine, the noise level was off the charts. Even loving every kid, critter, and snorer didn't keep me from often feeling like I was plugged into a high-voltage outlet with seemingly no outlet for my own feelings of failure, impatience, and bitchiness. Luckily, realizing how my nervous system and brain were wired gave me permission to begin setting boundaries that worked for me and weren't too restrictive for my family.

Because highly sensitive people gravitate to books like this, you may be an HSP. If so, it's especially important that you remain mindful of your sensitivity and take tender, consistent care of yourself without judgment. Even if you think you don't have a sensitive bone in your body or a sensitive emotion in your psyche, it's still absolutely essential that you are mindful of your own needs and care for yourself as well as you do others. In our troubled and troubling world, I wholeheartedly believe women are called to model kindness and well-being to the whole human race. And, of course, the best way to become such a model is to guard your own well-being as tenaciously and protectively as a loving mother would.

Feminine Qualities

Becoming mindful is an excellent avenue for self-care and self-realization. In order to get the most out of mindfulness, you need to practice it in ways that are harmonious with your basic nature. The practices contained in The Woman's Book of Mindfulness concentrate on feminine strengths, qualities, and energies.

The following list of feminine qualities and energies is by no means complete. Rather, it is a sampling pointing out the intuitive, relational heart of femininity.

Feminine qualities include:

Diffuse awareness: perceives and understands a wide range of stimuli simultaneously; expansive comprehension

Sensitive: responsive to external and internal conditions or stimulation; susceptible to attitudes, feelings, or circumstances of self and others

Emotionally grounded: steady, stable, well-balanced, able to bring all of her energy to exactly where she is in the moment

Intuitive: holistic, accessing immediate perception rather than rational thinking

Relational: interested in preserving and deepening relationships

Compassionate: empathetic, warm, openhearted, understanding

Empowered: with steeled softness, champions the weak and vulnerable and stands firm for what is right

Honoring of process: able to allow circumstances, ideas, and experiences to unfold

Gentle: able to live gently with herself and others

Forgiving: realizes we are all imperfect and that non-forgiveness dams the natural flow of life force

Receptive: open to receive the new, different, and wondrous

Introspective: drawn to the spiritual and philosophical

Strong: inherently able to overcome whatever life throws at her in order to accomplish what is needed

Healing: carries the ability to heal body, mind, and spirit through listening deeply to her internal, inherent wisdom

Recognizing these feminine qualities as ones you possess, or aspire to possess, can help you understand and respect the natural qualities you have and use them to lovingly and tolerantly guide yourself on a path to increased mindfulness.

PRACTICE: MINDFULLY INVITING A QUALITY THROUGH BREATHING

Although the following breath practice is very simple, it is incredibly effective. Using your breath mindfully will invite a quality to live within you, and as a result, you'll express it naturally through you.

If one of the qualities listed above resonates with your heart, choose it for the practice. If not, please select a different quality you would like to embrace. For instance, a few days ago I felt frustrated and thwarted by circumstances beyond my control; as a result, I was impatient beyond belief. Because of the way I felt, choosing to breathe in patience was a no-brainer.

Unlike some of the more meditative practices, this one can be done anywhere. I did it while driving. The simple steps are:

Choose a quality you would like to embody.

Become aware of your breath.

As you inhale, imagine the quality being drawn deeply into your body and spirit. (It sometimes helps to give the quality a color. For me, patience was a muted salmon color.)

As you exhale, breathe out any resistance you may be holding toward anything—the practice, the quality, circumstances, whatever…

Consciously and deeply breathe in your chosen quality for at least a few full breaths.

As I was driving while consciously breathing in patience, I became acutely aware of the panorama of the snow-covered Rocky Mountains ahead and felt as if the Divine Mother had gifted me with a beautiful example of stately patience. I like to imagine that beautiful vista as a reward for inviting a quality into myself I was sorely lacking at the time and as an affirmation that such mindful efforts can bring beautiful results.

We use the introspection and inspiration frequently found within mindfulness practices as a way to know ourselves more intimately and to thereby express ourselves in the world as we were created to do. Knowing yourself and being mindful of what your heart and soul long for and yearn to give is one of your highest callings. Philosopher Lao-tzu taught that, "Knowing others is wisdom, knowing yourself is Enlightenment." All you are and can be is within. Your life's mission is to pay attention and gently coax your unique authenticity into expression.

Insight is essential and can be exhilarating and very freeing. Gaining the insight that I was a highly sensitive person was both. However, in order to create enduring life changes and be the best and happiest woman you can be, insight needs to be accompanied by both mindful awareness and positive action. The practices you'll be introduced to are intended to strengthen that combination by using what I call the Insight to Awareness to Action progression:

Insight → Awareness → Action

BUSY WOMEN CAN BE MINDFUL TOO

Because women possess an innate ability to perceive an expanded range of feelings, thoughts, and experiences, we are adept at consciously handling several things at once. That doesn't mean you don't get frazzled and frustrated. It does mean you can feel even better and more productive by attentively, purposely, and nonjudgmentally staying in the present moment. Having qualities such as diffuse awareness and sensitivity means you already possess excellent tools for creating a more peaceful, loving, and mindful life. With awareness and intention, you can be mindful within your busyness. The caveat is that your state of busyness needs to be comfortable and enjoyable, not fear-based, frantic action. We'll explore both forms of busyness in various practices throughout the book.

INTENTION AS ALLY

Your thoughts and intentions announce your deepest wishes, desires, and goals to your subconscious mind, or Inner Sage, whose job it is to bring you more of what you project. It's great to have so willing a friend as long as your thoughts are positive and your intentions are set purposefully. So often, however, they are neither. Many of our thoughts and intentions reflect deep-seated fears, unhealthy beliefs, and intolerances. For instance, if we fear we're not up to snuff in our job and think things like, "Good grief, how dense can I be?!" or "I'm never going to be able to learn all this!" sure enough our brain, mind, and subconscious centers will obligingly provide what we prescribed—feelings of inadequacy and stupidity. And, of course, such feelings make it hard for us to concentrate and keep us from learning as quickly and easily as we could if we were free from fear. Or if we believe we're being treated unfairly, we may gnaw on feelings of being cheated and long for revenge; then once again the Inner Sage will cooperatively present matching experiences and feelings.

Luckily, thoughts and intentions are equal opportunity magnets. Actually, I choose to believe they are tipped slightly toward the love and joy side of the equation. Yes, we can attract negatives, but our benevolent inner universe really seems to want to give us the good stuff more than it does the difficult. Consequently, thoughts of love, tolerance, acceptance, and general goodwill combined with conscious, positive intentions draw more good to us than we can even imagine. On the other hand, unhealthy, fear-based thoughts and intentions draw to us more of the same. Henry Ford was right when he said, "Whether we think we can or think we can't, we're right."

It's important to know that your subconscious mind is extremely literal and unable to discern between "true" and "false," "good" and "bad," or "positive" and "negative." What you say, believe, think, fear, and assume, the subconscious will do its darnedest to provide. The wonderful news is that knowing the nature of your Inner Sage gives you the understanding and ability to use the power of positivity to mindfully set life-enhancing intentions that will unerringly help you become a magnet for your desired results.

Intentions can be both expansive and minute. You can set far-reaching intentions such as, "My intention is to be a mindful woman," or intentions for the moment like, "My intention is to pay absolute attention to my next four breaths."

Expansive: My intention is to become more loving.

Minute: I chose to respond (or stay silent) lovingly to _____right now.

Expansive: My intention is to be a healthy weight for my body type.

Minute: I am choosing to forego this piece of candy right now.

Intention is an invaluable ally on your journey toward increased mindfulness. One small step that can make a huge difference is to set an intention each morning before you are off and running. I might say, "Today I will be consistently kind." Or if I'm worried about someone I love, one of my favorite intentions or affirmations is, "I place _____in the arms of angels today and know that s/he is loved and protected."

Intentions are like personal angels who set our course and light the way to where we want to go and how we want to be in our lives, loves, and attitudes. Of course, because we're human beings, we'll fall short of our intentions time and again. When we do, it's important to take an accepting, angelic approach and love ourselves back into alignment. Gentle correction is much more effective than criticism and judgment.

WHY CHOOSE MINDFULNESS?

Mindfulness is one of the most effective tools we can use to create more user-friendly brains. Have you ever noticed how easily your mind holds onto negative emotions and fixates on unhappy experiences? Have you seen how much it loves to gnaw on hurtful scenarios and pick at the scabs of old wounds? I have. And I've felt really guilty and discouraged by it. So it is with great relief and joy that I welcome current brain research showing that although our brain/mind complex is wired to emphasize negative experiences, it can be taught to register positive experiences more deeply and quickly. Goodbye guilt, hello retraining.

Retraining the Brain

While there is an abundance of research on the brain/mind system, my main source for the following information is from the workshop Awakening Your Brain: Tools for Meditative Depth, Peacefulness, Happiness, and Equanimity, led by Rick Hanson, PhD, and Rick Mendius, MD. Dr. Hanson is a psychologist and Dr. Mendius is a neurologist; as such, they are well equipped to provide information and insight on both the physical/medical and emotional/spiritual aspects of the brain and mind, which they see as one unified system.

Although the scope of The Woman's Book of Mindfulness does not permit a comprehensive exploration of Dr. Hanson and Dr. Mendius's research, with their permission, I have highlighted a simplified version of two points which are especially relevant to our quest for mindfulness. I view the first as a 'good news, bad news' scenario.

The Brain/Mind Emphasizes Negative Experiences

The "bad" news is that Mother Nature has wired our brains to register negative, fearful, and unpleasant experiences more deeply and vividly than it does positive, neutral, or pleasant ones. Why? Because she wants grandchildren. Therefore, we—her children—are programmed to survive above all else. Since negative experiences are more central to the survival of the species, they generally eclipse positive experiences. As an example, Dr. Hanson says, "A single bad event with a dog is more memorable than a thousand good experiences. The brain is like Velcro for negative experiences and Teflon for positive."

So where is the "good" news in this discovery? For me, this research answers my questions about why it's so easy to go into an emotional slump, be in a bad mood, obsess over slights, or descend into any number of other self-sabotaging behaviors and thought patterns. These patterns can seduce me away from my own happiness, peace of mind, and my ability to love openheartedly and experience life with joyous and grateful abandon. Knowing my brain is wired for survival helps me understand that God/Mother Nature is simply trying to protect me by creating its wiring that way.

And that leads to more good news. There is absolutely no reason to feel guilty or ashamed if we tilt in a downer direction now and then. As a psychotherapist, friend, and woman, it's been my experience that most women have a tendency to default to an at-fault position. If something goes wrong or someone is unhappy—including ourselves—we have a tendency to think, "What did I do wrong?" Simply knowing of our brains' propensity to accentuate the negative, we can breathe a collective sigh of relief and gently let ourselves off the blame/shame hook.

The best news of all is that we can retrain our brains to better absorb and savor positive, 'upper' experiences, beliefs, thoughts, and feelings.

Positive Experiences Are Best Registered in the Brain through Conscious Attention

Sounds familiar, doesn't it? In fact, many of the avenues we will take on our journey toward making mindfulness a habit are strikingly similar to those Drs. Hanson and Mendius endorse in their workshop. Their research affirms that mindfulness offers us wonderful ways to befriend our brains and retrain our minds to attract and accept increased joy, peace, health, and relaxation.

It is a loving and practical choice to choose mindfulness because:

Mindfulness adds value and meaning to life.

Mindfulness helps you inhabit your life, thereby engaging and enjoying it more fully.

Mindfulness calms your spirit, quiets your mind, and opens your heart.

Mindfulness helps you feel you are on the right path—that you are doing life well and being who you are meant to be.

Mindfulness brings out the best in you.

Mindfulness relaxes your body.

Mindfulness retrains your brain.

Mindfulness enhances appreciation and gratitude.

Mindfulness helps you break unhealthy habits.

Mindfulness invites balance and harmony.

Mindfulness enhances humor.

Mindfulness minimizes scatteredness.

Mindfulness helps you love yourself and others more deeply and freely.

BENEFITS OF MINDFULNESS

Even though my dad described my infant self as "an eel with insomnia," and even though I can still sometimes be fueled by uncomfortably distracted energy, the stretches of mindfulness I am able to sustain, no matter how momentary at times, are creating a quieter and more peaceful mind. The patter of regrets, what-ifs, shame, and worry that used to plague me are mostly replaced by a softer attitude full of gratitude, contentment, and joy. My old habits of doing too much, resting too little, and putting myself last are transforming into healthy habits of self-care.

Among the most relaxing and grace-filled benefits I'm receiving from mindfulness are those of compassionate nonattachment, letting be, and lightening up, which are discussed in greater depth in Part III. Even after practicing mindfulness for a relatively short time, I was completely surprised and totally gratified when it gave me the courage and ability to let go of situations that had weighed heavily on me for years and develop compassionate nonattachment. The ability to lovingly let be is a very pleasant and freeing bonus and one that other mindful women have shared they also enjoy.

I credit a gentle, small steps approach to mindfulness practice with bringing more simplicity, love, freedom, and awareness into my mind, heart, and life.

Although we are not monks, but busy women comfortably able to multitask much of the time, we have the wonderful ability to make our lives and hearts even happier and more joyous by learning to be increasingly mindful in a feminine way.

Because you already lead full and often complicated lives, I've designed the practices in the rest of the book around a core of small, doable steps. The practices are simple; hopefully they will entice you into regular, ever-expanding times of mindful presence. They issue an invitation to relax, revitalize, and reconnect with the essence of yourself and what makes life meaningful to you. Each practice was developed to help you overcome distractions and strengthen your habit of mindfulness. They encourage you to be gentle with yourself as you move ever more surely toward enjoying the benefits to be gained from mindfulness. The practices can be as long or short as you like. Mainly, I hope you find them fun and effective. They are meant to be enjoyed.

Be gentle with yourself as you embark on or expand your mindfulness journey, and please remember that we all—even the masters among us—are still practicing.

In a Nutshell

Feminine qualities such as sensitivity and diffuse awareness make women uniquely suited to the practice of mindfulness.

Mindfulness is being nonjudgmentally aware of self and circumstances in the present moment and fully engaged in the here and now.

Four essential elements of mindfulness are: Paying Attention; Inhabiting the Moment; Simplifying; and Breathing.

Although our brains are built to accentuate the negative, they can be retrained to better attract and absorb the positive.

We intentionally choose to practice mindful living because the benefits from doing so makes us happier, kinder, more relaxed, and more fulfilled.

A few mindful moments make a world of difference.

PART II
The Practices

Chapter 2

Cultivating Compassionate Awareness

"Compassion for others begins with kindness to ourselves."

—Pema Chodron

For years, I have been teaching and writing that kindness toward ourselves is not only acceptable, but actually an incubator for increased compassion toward others. Nonetheless, the above quote from Pema Chodron, an American Buddhist nun and teacher, still touches me. Her message that compassion for others is born from kindness to ourselves soothes the part of my psyche still valiantly trying to avoid the childhood admonition, "Don't be so selfish!" Because I and many women I talk with seem to need at least intermittent reassurance that self-care is not synonymous with selfishness, the majority of the practices in this chapter are reminders to treat yourself as kindly and compassionately as you do others.

In order to treat yourself with consistent compassion and kindness, you need to be aware of what is happening in and around you. All insight and change begin with awareness. Without awareness, your choices are limited and it's easy to get caught in the trap of repeating old habits and rehashing ancient hurts. However, being aware of what you are thinking and feeling enables you to intentionally, gently, and lovingly choose to change attitudes and actions that are no longer appropriate or desired.

Compassionate awareness is the cornerstone of mindfulness. With awareness, you become deeply attuned to yourself and increasingly appreciative of the people, opportunities, and, yes, the challenges life offers. Awareness is the first step toward both inner and outer change.

BEGINNING WITH BREATH

The first thing you ever did for yourself was breathe. In order to enter into this life, you needed to take that first breath, no matter how scary or unfamiliar it felt to do so. And consciously focusing on your breath remains the epitome of self-care throughout your entire life. Breath is both starter and sustainer.

Have you ever noticed feeling tight and constricted when experiencing stress, overwhelm, or worry? Even during minor upsets, we tend to pull into ourselves like turtles retreating to the safety of their shells. In order to protect ourselves, we unconsciously get as small, compact, and hard as possible, which naturally leads to shallow, restricted breathing. The best thing you can do for yourself when you notice you're barely breathing is to take a few deep, cleansing breaths.

We have a dogleg driveway that makes getting in and out of the garage pretty tricky. The other day, I was cautiously backing my relatively new car out while concentrating hard on clearing both the garage door and the neighbor's fence behind me. When I had safely accomplished that feat, my husband chuckled and said, "Breathe, Susie." He was absolutely right; I had all but stopped breathing. His reminder made me laugh and take a deep breath.

It's ironic that our impulse to close down and constrict breathing during both mini and major crises is exactly the opposite of helpful. Shallow breathing depletes your resources, while breathing deeply oxygenates your brain, grounds you in your body, and maximizes your mental, emotional, and physical capabilities.

In mindfulness practice, breath is an ever-present mainstay, a maypole around which our thoughts and feelings can flutter and whip. Simply by reminding yourself to breathe, you can replace a detrimental, automatic reaction with a healthy one.

PRACTICE...

- Before getting out of bed, intentionally focus on your breath.

- Take at least seven deep, conscious breaths.

- Thank your breath for faithfully sustaining you from the first moment of your life until now.

THROUGHOUT YOUR DAY...

· Become aware of your breath and express gratitude for it.

Return to breath.

STOPPING TO LOOK, LISTEN, AND FEEL

Louise, a client of mine, was a sleepwalker who came to see me because she had awakened in the middle of the night about a block away from her home. To make matters worse, she had locked herself out. Trying to attract her partner's attention without waking the whole neighborhood convinced her she needed to find a cure for her perplexing malady. As a psychotherapist, I was part of her support system while she waded through various medical doctors and medicines. Together we found a few exercises that cut her sleepwalking episodes in half. One was a simple awareness practice.

We started small. Before falling asleep, Louise affirmed, "I will wake up while I'm still in the house." Of course, she and her partner also augmented the intentions and medications with practical tools like chairs in front of the doors. As she progressed, her affirmation of awareness became, "I will wake up before I get out of bed." And she did. With practice and patience, Louise was ultimately able to stop all medication and sleep normally most of the time.

I couldn't help noticing how similar my own daytime rushing and that of other clients was to Louise's subconscious nighttime meanderings. Without conscious commitment, awareness, and practice, it's easy to sleep-live our lives away. In order to awaken from the autopilot activity of sleep-living and savor life to the fullest, it's important to Stop, Look, Listen, and Feel. Because it's a shift in attitude and focus, the practice of stop-look-listen-feel can be done quickly at any time and in anyplace; while ironing, working at the computer, making love, cleaning the litter box, in class, dancing, cooking, driving…

Pausing to take note of what you're seeing, hearing, and feeling is an incredibly important touchstone for mindful living. A few sixty-second check-ins a day can make an amazing difference in how you feel and lay valuable groundwork for building mindful habits. As with all the practices, it's important to lovingly and gently accept and embrace what you discover.

PRACTICE...

- Become aware when you have fallen into sleep-living. (This may be the hardest part of the practice until you become accustomed to being aware of yourself.)

- Wake up to what you are seeing. What beauty is there to appreciate right now?

- Listen to the sounds around you. Identify one for which you are thankful.

- Check on your feelings. Is a feeling calling attention to itself? If so, breathe deeply into the part of your body holding the feeling. Love the feeling even if you would rather avoid or resist it.

THROUGHOUT YOUR DAY...

- After each check-in, express—and feel, if you can—gratitude for the gifts of sight, hearing, and feeling.

With loving kindness, pause to look, listen, and feel.

PAYING ATTENTION TO WARNING SIGNS

Although it's easy to forget to pay attention to ourselves, not doing so can be a potential killer. Marie, a young woman whom I love, is a single mother with two little girls, one biological and one adopted from overseas. Between a stressful fulltime job that includes the expense and worry of work-related travel and her deep love of and commitment to parenting the girls and supporting their differing emotional needs, Marie fell into the habit of sticking self-care on the back burner.

Even after months of insomnia and several anxiety attacks, Marie continued to put her own needs after those of her children and her work. Luckily, the intense chest pains and inability to breathe that eventually sent her to the Emergency Room were not a heart attack. Actually, the ER visit was a blessing, because Marie made the commitment to make herself a priority. And she has been true to her promise since then.

A former athlete, Marie has returned to running and other forms of exercise that promote her physical, mental, and emotional well-being. She no longer indulges in stress eating but consciously makes a choice for health before eating. After the first two weeks of her self-care commitment, Marie said, "The first week was tough, but I no longer want to make poor choices, and I already love me more!" She's become much more aware of her body's warning signs. Now when she feels her heart flutter, she takes an emotional and mental step back, breathes, and reminds herself of what's truly important to her. By listening to and lovingly responding to her body, the fluttering in her heart has never again escalated.

After congratulating Marie, I asked, "What helps you the most in keeping your commitment to yourself?" Without hesitation, she replied, "Paying attention."

PRACTICE...

- Take a few minutes to pay attention to the way your body feels.

- Without judgment, breathe deeply into any troublesome area.

- As you support the uncomfortable areas of your body with breath, ask them what they need from you. Responses may be so subtle that it's necessary to engage your intuition to discern what your body wants and needs.

THROUGHOUT YOUR DAY...

- Reaffirm your intention to pay attention to your body and take care of its needs.

You deserve to make yourself a priority.

SHOWERING YOURSELF
WITH STARS

Along with the brain-mind complex being wired to accentuate the negative as we discussed in Chapter 1, our self-assessments tend to be tilted toward the critical rather than the appreciative. I know I can gnaw on a comment I wish I hadn't made like a hungry buzzard ripping apart a carcass. And I can also feel like dead meat after a bout of such self-criticism. Because it bothers me so much, I usually do a reality check with people I fear I may have hurt. Often, the people I think I've wounded don't even remember me doing or saying anything. Or if they do and were upset, they are quick to understand and forgive.

We can learn a lot from those who are quick to understand and forgive, and as a result, we can then commit to being generous and forgiving with ourselves. In fact, many of us probably need to take it a step further and make a commitment to concentrate on appreciating what we do and say or refrain from doing and saying. We can break the habit of criticizing ourselves and skimming over most of the loving, wise, and witty things we do and say. One lighthearted way to break the criticism habit is to accentuate and underscore the positive by giving ourselves actual gold stars for even the smallest accomplishment. For instance, if you are wrestling with depression or grief, you may gold star yourself for getting out of bed that day. If the kids are driving you crazy, you deserve at least one gold star for not raising your voice even though you feel like running from the house screaming, returning only to put them up for sale on eBay.

Appreciation is an oil that lubricates life and keeps our wheels turning easily and freely. Without appreciation, wheels can still turn, but they are apt to become rusted with resentment and exhaustion. Since there is great truth in the well-known statement "We teach people how to treat us," you can start teaching others to shower you with appreciation by showering yourself with it first.

PRACTICE...

- Buy yourself gold star stickers—the bigger, the better.

- Have fun appreciating yourself, and do so with over-the-top generosity.

- Each day, give yourself one or more gold stars for:

  - ☒ ...something you said
  - ☒ ...something you did
  - ☒ ...something you wisely left unsaid or undone

THROUGHOUT YOUR DAY...

- Give at least one other person a verbal (or actual) gold star.

You teach others to appreciate you by first appreciating yourself.

TAKING TIME-OUTS

While many younger women may never have heard them, I was raised on a myriad of expressions like "Idle hands are the devil's workshop," "A man may work from sun to sun, but a woman's work is never done," and "It's good to stay as busy as a beaver." As a child, I must have taken the implied lessons in these platitudes to heart, because for most of my adult life, it was next to impossible to give myself permission to take a break during daylight hours. I was so brainwashed by those childhood sayings that I often overlooked blatant signals I had run out of steam and needed to take a break. As a result, I was often overtired, overworked, and overwhelmed, not to mention feeling royally ticked off at those around me who were being mindful and honoring of their own energy levels.

My dear friend Bonnie is a person who rests, and consequently, she earned my ire early in our relationship. Her ability to rest eventually taught me incredibly valuable lessons about the art of taking time-outs. To this day, Bonnie is astutely aware of times when her energy dips too low and resolutely honors her need to rest. To boost her energy, she's been known to sit quietly with a cup of tea, adjourn a workshop we were cofacilitating to take a five-minute breather, or slip out of her own wedding reception to be restored by a few minutes of solitude in the sun. Before I could admit how absolutely horrible I was at paying attention to and honoring my own energy depletion, I projected onto Bonnie all the labels I was afraid would be pasted on me if I allowed myself to take rejuvenating time-outs. The fear of being thought selfish, rude, self-indulgent, or lazy kept me from being mindful of my own needs.

Although my brain had known for a long time that overdoing drained my reserves and that rest was good for me, awareness of this principle only sank into my gut when I made a commitment to self-compassion and self-care. Of course, there are times when we simply need to choose to tough it out and do what needs doing. Remembering to breathe deeply, with

awareness, during tough-it-out times is immeasurably helpful. Also helpful
is making sure you balance stressful, energy-draining times with restful and
restorative interludes.

PRACTICE...

- In stressful situations, remind yourself to breathe and repeat, "I love
  myself... I love myself."

- As soon as your energy dips below your comfort level, take a five- or
  ten-minute time-out. Breathe deeply and turn your face to the sun,
  if possible.

- If you cannot take a time-out, put your hand over your heart and
  sense or feel its beating. Thank it.

THROUGHOUT YOUR DAY...

- Refresh yourself with at least three short, rejuvenating time-outs.

Have the courage to allow yourself time-outs.

UNCOVERING THE ORIGIN OF FEELING

The most profound agents of creation are invisible. The two that spring to mind are God and thought. We enjoy the benefits and beauty of God's creations each moment and reap the fruits of our thoughts throughout our entire lives. Whether our thoughts produce sweet or sour fruit is entirely up to us. It is a great kindness to fully embrace the idea that your thoughts are the origin of your feelings. Why? Because you have total control over your own thoughts, and consequently, you have the power to choose those that bring you happiness and discard those that don't.

Imagine your mind as a garden and your thoughts as the seeds you plant. Habitual negative, unhealthy, self-critical thoughts produce the weeds and thistles of depression, discontent, and anxiety. Luckily, the opposite is also true. Consistently planting positive, healthy, constructive thoughts will yield a crop of beautiful feelings such as gratitude, love, and joy.

The hardest part of changing thought patterns is being aware of noxious thoughts before they sprout into full-blown negative feelings. Unhealthy thinking is a stubborn habit, often one we've built up over a lifetime. However, with patience and perseverance, it is a habit we can break.

Uncovering and altering the origins of weedlike feelings is a process I've been practicing for decades, yet I still needed to do some pretty hefty pruning just this week. Due to family circumstances not of my own making, though nonetheless time and energy-consuming, I found myself feeling resentful, impatient, and definitely less-than-loving. In short, I was feeling bitchy and put-upon.

Thoughts such as "Good grief, yet another interruption in my writing process" and "When am I going to have the time for my own life and projects?" were generating feelings of 'poor me, poor little ol' beleaguered me.'

Having uncovered the culprit thoughts, I changed them to positive, grateful ones like "How lucky I am to have family to care for" and "I have all the time and energy I need to complete this book." It worked. After a little while, poor me became lucky me, and the feelings changed accordingly.

PRACTICE...

- When a painful or angry feeling arises, notice it without judgment.

- Gently uncover the thought or thoughts creating the feeling.

- Even if it seems too simplistic to be helpful, choose to consciously change the negative thought to a positive one.

THROUGHOUT YOUR DAY...

- Repeat the positive thought you have chosen each time the negative one sneaks back into your mind.

Thinking is the origin of feeling.

RECOGNIZING EMOTIONAL FALLOUT

Whenever I begin writing a book, the Imperial Imp in charge of writers in early stages of projects seems to think it would be great fun to have me act, feel, and express exactly the opposite of my current topic. When starting my first book, The Courage to Be Yourself, I could have won the Appeaser of the Year award, and at the beginning of Heart Centered Marriage, everything my husband did grated on my nerves.

True to form, when I was originally organizing The Woman's Book of Mindfulness, I was so scattered that I began calling myself Dr. Ditzy, even though I knew that was lousy self-talk. Although my lack of focus for everything except the book was a little amusing, it was also really frustrating. My fuse kept getting shorter and shorter until I completely lost my temper when the cat rode my treasured antique bamboo birdcage down the stairs for the umpteenth time. Wisely, cat, dog, and man all disappeared to safer rooms and I was left steaming and storming (and picking up shards of bamboo) all by myself.

Recognizing that losing my temper was playing all sorts of havoc with my physical and emotional bodies, I took a drive to assess the emotional fallout. Because I'm basically allergic to being enraged, I needed to reassure my churning stomach, constricted throat, and shamed inner child that everything was okay and that we were okay even though angry. As I was getting out of the car to get a coke, I accidentally rammed my hand into the steering wheel, tearing my fingernail off past the quick. My initial response was unprintable until I noticed which finger was injured: the middle one, of course! Until the fingernail grew back, I had a humorous reminder that for me, giving in to anger and expressing it in less than constructive ways is not worth the emotional fallout.

In reality, thoughts create feelings, and feelings create both internal and external consequences. It's up to us to recognize which of our feelings are toxic and which are uplifting. With that awareness, we can mindfully and gently choose how to respond when feelings arise. Of course, we won't always choose well, but reassuring and loving ourselves can usually help free us from emotional fallout.

PRACTICE...

- After giving in to a strong feeling, assess its effect on your body, mind, and emotions.

- If you are pleased with the aftereffects, give yourself a gold star.

- If you are not pleased, love yourself through your disappointment and set an intention to respond differently next time around.

THROUGHOUT YOUR DAY...

- Choose self-loving actions and responses.

You are a worthwhile and lovable woman even though you experience uncomfortable feelings.

ACCEPTING RATHER THAN REJECTING

Have you ever noticed that you can change personalities to fit a mood or occasion as readily as you change clothes to suit the weather? One moment you can be an in-charge career woman, next a loving mom or friend, and then you might morph into the Wicked Witch of the West. If that is true for you, you're not crazy, you're simply moving between aspects of yourself as circumstances and feelings dictate. We all have several aspects, or subpersonalities, active within us at any given time. Some subpersonalities are healthier, happier, and more mature than others. You can begin to enjoy all aspects of yourself by becoming aware of who's in charge in the moment, asking what they want and need, and then loving them to wholeness through acceptance.

Rose, a client, shared that during a meeting in which two people were monopolizing everyone's time with inappropriate comments and jokes, she asked the part of herself feeling irritated and impatient, "What subpersonality are you?" In her mind's eye, Rose then saw a spiky-haired cartoon character with crossed eyes and jangling nerves shooting out of her head. In answer to the question, "What do you want?" the character snapped, "I want them to shut up!" (What is wanted is often a surface response, whereas what is needed is usually a core desire for subpersonalities.) When Rose asked, "What do you need?" the response was, "I just need you to understand how crazy all this jabbering is making me." Rose could easily oblige, and in the theater of her mind, she nurtured her subpersonality by smoothing down her nerve-hairs, calming and holding her, and most importantly, accepting her. It worked, and as a result, Rose was able to make it through the rest of the meeting with a modicum of serenity.

We are always choosing between personalities. For instance, even if you were having an absolute melt-down, you would immediately switch to a helper personality if an injured child needed you. Becoming aware of your subpersonalities in order to consciously choose between them is incredibly empowering. Accepting and understanding your subpersonalities gives them an environment in which they can heal, transform, and express the positive qualities inherent within them.

PRACTICE...

- Become acquainted with one subpersonality this week. Name her.

- Ask her what she wants and needs from you.

- To the best of your ability, give her what she needs.

THROUGHOUT YOUR DAY...

- Give your various subpersonalities a pat on the back or a hug.

Each aspect of yourself is inherently valuable and worthwhile.

LIVING GENTLY
WITH YOURSELF

What a wondrous kaleidoscope of contradictions, idiosyncrasies, and lovable qualities we women are. Many of the paradoxes and quirks we display actually serve to make us fun and interesting to be around. However, one contradiction that can only breed low self-esteem and often depression is treating others with gentleness while heaping judgment on ourselves. You deserve and need your own gentle support and definitely thrive best when you are your own trustworthy cheerleader.

Many years ago, I came up with the motto Live gently with yourself and others because I needed to learn that lesson myself. Because I continue to need reminders, my business cards have sported the maxim since the days when I was my only client, and my license plate reads LVGNTLY.

I believe one of our souls' major purposes is to know, love, and express our authentic selves—to live the life we were meant to live and be the person we were created to be. However, our true selves will only emerge when it's safe to do so. Self-condemnation, shame, guilt, and judgment send your true nature into hiding. It is only in the safety of gentle curiosity, support, encouragement, and self-love that your soul can bloom as it was created to do. If I am right about our souls' purpose, it's not only loving to treat ourselves gently, but also a spiritual responsibility.

Please treat yourself gently today, always, and in all ways. It is the wise and soulful thing to do.

PRACTICE...

- Set an intention to treat yourself gently and respectfully.

- If you become aware of treating yourself harshly, pause, take a centering breath or two, and thank yourself for noticing.

- Consciously return to treating yourself gently.

- It's okay to ask a friend or mate to help remind you to be gentle with yourself. My husband Gene says, "Is that gentle self-talk, Susie?" when I stray. (Although it can be kind of annoying, it's helpful and usually makes me laugh.)

THROUGHOUT YOUR DAY...

- Ask yourself, "Is this a gentle way to act, respond, or talk to myself?" If the answer is no, choose a gentler way.

Gentleness invites your soul to soar.

_____

INVITING AWARENESS THROUGH HAIKU

Creativity of all kinds focuses your mind, engages your imagination, and feeds your soul. Being creative can also facilitate understanding and encourage healing. Creativity is mindfulness in motion—intuitive, artistic motion. Creative moments and activities give you a boost and help you feel energized and good about yourself.

One creative endeavor I simply love is writing haiku poems. Haiku is a type of poetry from the Japanese culture. It is simple, compact, and can include themes of nature, feelings, and experiences. A haiku has only three lines and rarely rhymes. The first line has five syllables, the second line seven syllables, and the third line five syllables. The fun and challenge of haiku is painting a mental picture in only three lines using a scant seventeen syllables.

Haiku offers a process of simplifying and distilling that invites new awareness and deeper understanding into our hearts and minds. For instance, when our family was experiencing a fissure over religious differences years ago, I wrote my first haiku at a workshop and sang it in front of a room full of people.

> Wolves together stand
>
> Howling soft and loud at light.
>
> Singing family songs.

For reasons I've never fully been able to articulate, that little poem took much of the sting out of a trying period in our lives. Each time I started to obsess over the situation, I chose to sing my haiku and felt better.

PRACTICE...

- If you are feeling resistant to writing a haiku, which one of your subpersonalities is balking? Encourage and support that aspect of yourself in whatever way it needs.

- Play with writing a haiku even if part of you is resisting.

Five syllables

_____

Seven syllables

_____

Five syllables

_____

Throughout your day...

- Do something creative one or more times. (It doesn't have to be haiku.)

Becoming aware,

Live gently with yourself by

Writing a haiku.

_____

Being at Home in the Moment

"If we could see the miracle of a single flower clearly, our whole life would change."

—Buddha

I vividly remember a time when I completely understood what the Buddha meant about seeing the miracle of a single flower being life changing. My husband Gene and I had a transoceanic courtship spanning the Pacific. To help bridge the miles, he once sent me red roses. After my sons were asleep, I took the time to luxuriate in every aspect of the fullest rose, exploring its textures and colors and the varying shapes of petals, stem, and stamen. To my surprise, tears of joy began to slip from my eyes, and I felt enveloped in love and connected to both the man who sent the roses and to their creator as well.

Although my rapt attention to the flower was the act of a young woman wildly in love, the experience of it has become an enduring touchstone reminding me of the power and joy a few mindful moments can bring. Decades later, I clearly remember that particular rose and can revisit the profound sense of wonder and awe I experienced while focusing on it.

Obviously, not all our moments are coming up roses. In fact, many of them are extremely painful and sad. No matter what it contains, the moment is still our home. As the noted Vietnamese monk Thích Nhất Hanh says, "The present moment is where life can be found, and if you don't arrive there, you miss your appointment with life." As well as highlighting happy moments, the practice of mindfulness can help us find glimmers of understanding, gratitude, peace, and hope in even the most difficult times.

By being mindfully at home in the moment, we keep our appointment with life.

TAMING THE MONKEY MIND

While living in Hawaii, we visited a restaurant that boasted a Monkey Bar. Behind the bartender and rows of liquor bottles was a glass partition, shielding patrons from the smell and splatters of the countless monkeys living there. Their relentless chatter (which could be heard dully through the partition), unceasing motion, and restless picking at each other made me acutely uncomfortable. Not only did I feel sorry for the monkeys, but their actions stirred up something in me that made it impossible to relax and enjoy dinner.

Talking with a client a few days later, the answer to my upset popped out of my mouth unbidden. While discussing her feelings of anxiety, I said, "It sounds like your mind was chattering away at you as chaotically as the monkeys at the Pearl City Monkey Bar do." Bingo! A big reason I was disturbed by those caged little monkeys was they provided a visceral reminder of how easily I could be imprisoned by my own restless and agitated mind chatter.

Having seen the Monkey Bar inhabitants up close, it makes total sense that the term "monkey mind" has become a colloquialism, especially within contemplative communities. However, I believe "monkey-minded" doesn't apply only to those who try to meditate but is a reflection of the scattered nature of our culture as well.

In order to stop the stress of thinking and doing too much at once, it's important to notice when thoughts and/or actions begin to disrupt each other and you start to feel frazzled. The very beginning of frazzledness is the time to gently and lovingly return to the moment. When your mind is overfull and flighty, it's easy to get sucked into a whirling vortex of responsibility, obligation, and stress. Overwhelmed by such uncomfortable feelings, it's easy to miss any peace and beauty that may be available in the current moment.

Mindfulness helps you to be fully present to your authentic self and to live your life with acute awareness and an open heart. An essential way to help open your heart more fully is to be patient and kind to yourself, even when your monkey mind seems incorrigible. Maintaining a patient attitude is easier when we remember what long-term mindfulness practitioners remain adamant about: taming our monkey-minds is generally an ongoing, lifelong learning process.

PRACTICE...

- Simply notice when your mind is leaping about distractedly and chattering incessantly.

- Without judgment, name what you notice. "My mind is chattering like crazy right now."

- Choose a single positive thought and repeat it several times.

- If your mind wanders, gently return your attention to your chosen thought.

THROUGHOUT YOUR DAY...

- Give yourself a mental attagirl each time you notice and refocus mind chatter.

Gift yourself with encouragement.

CHOOSING A POSITIVE ATTITUDE

I was overwhelmingly touched by the attitude of a young couple I met while volunteering as a hospice chaplain. I visited their home because Jim, the husband, was in the last stages of cancer and they wanted to talk about his eventual memorial service. Because they were a young couple with kids, I was anticipating a somber, grief-stricken atmosphere. I was wrong. Jim's wife, Morgan, greeted me at the door with a smile and said, "Hi, come on in. The house is kinda chaotic cause the kids are at the tail end of a sleepover and on a sugar high." With the exception of the gaunt young man lying on a hospital bed in the living room, the energy of both house and inhabitants was exactly what you'd expect from one brimming with sleep-deprived, sugar-stimulated kids—loud, boisterous, and happy.

Over the course of the next few weeks, Jim and Morgan taught me many lessons about appreciating each moment and looking on the bright side of things. Of course they had their down times, and she had fears about the loneliness of a life without Jim and how she could be both Mom and Dad to the kids. But underneath every joy and each heartache was an incredible stability and a belief that life was good. After several weeks, I asked how they maintained such a positive attitude. Both credited their parents for teaching them to accentuate the positive and look for the good, happy, and beautiful in everything. "It's just become second nature," Jim explained a few days before he died.

Although many of us probably didn't get such a thorough early education in the value of a positive attitude, we can teach ourselves. Simply by making a decision to look for the good, happy, and beautiful in all things and all people, you will have completed the first and most important step in learning to accentuate the positive. As with any new knowledge, it's best to start with the fundamentals and not overwhelm yourself by expecting to learn everything perfectly by tomorrow. Start slowly and gently keep on keeping on.

PRACTICE...

- Set an intention to be more positive and look for the good, happy, and beautiful within all experiences and people (including yourself).

- Jot your intention down in a place where you'll see it often. Visual reminders enhance intention.

- Before going to sleep, remind yourself of the positive things, thoughts, and feelings you experienced during the day.

THROUGHOUT YOUR DAY...

- Every few hours, look for the good, happy, or beautiful in one thing, person, experience, or bit of nature.

A positive attitude lightens your heart.

ENJOYING EVERYDAY BEAUTY

The universe is extremely generous. Beauty abounds in the most surprising locales and within even the most soul-searing experiences. We simply need to look for beauty and take the time to appreciate and digest what we see. I agree with Margaret Wolfe Hungerford's quote: "Beauty is in the eye of the beholder," but I would add that beauty is also in the beholder's desire and ability to see.

The other night, I was gifted with an unexpected beauty when I took our little dog, Lily, out to her piddle place, a fenced area beside the house. It is hidden from the road and "landscaped" meagerly with rocks. Its sole decoration is the garbage can. Expecting the same old bedtime routine, I was blessed by beauty instead. The streetlight, which goes on and off sporadically, was backlighting the brand-new, fuzzy catkins on our neighbors' aspen tree. They looked as if they were encased in sparkling ice, shimmering and dancing in the early spring breeze. An awed "Ahhhhhh" escaped as I exhaled. While Lily did what she was supposed to do, I turned off our light, inked the beauty of the backlit catkins in my mind's eye, and whispered a prayer of gratitude for a lovely surprise in such an everyday place and action.

While the beauty of the illuminated aspen would have been hard to ignore, I easily could have done just that before making the promise to myself to lead a more mindful, appreciative, and in-the-moment life.

In order to enjoy everyday beauty, we need a desire to see it and the willingness to open our hearts to it. It helps when we go about our days expecting to be blessed by beauty at every turn. Our expectations and how we pay attention to the beauty of the moment magnetizes loveliness to us. Appreciating and reveling in beauty can soothe your soul, relax your body, and immerse you in gratitude.

PRACTICE...

- Expect to find beauty in the strangest places.

- Enjoy and appreciate the beauty you notice.

- Really see and appreciate an aspect of your own beauty.

THROUGHOUT YOUR DAY...

- Notice miniscule moments of Mother Nature's magic.

Beauty is in the eye of the beholder expecting to see it.

SURROUNDING WITH SPACE

Just for fun, where did your eyes first go when looking at this page? If it was to the sentence encircled in white space, you already know the point of this practice.

Space enhances that which it surrounds.

Artists, musicians, parents, decorators, public speakers, animal trainers, florists, and actors are among the many people who know the value of accentuating their art with silence and space. Any of you who have framed (or even admired) a photograph or written an invitation in calligraphy know about calling attention to the focal point by surrounding it with space. Art galleries leave space between paintings to allow viewers to concentrate on one piece at a time. And musicians, including church choir director Kamilla Macar, say it is the interplay between sound and silence that helps make music meaningful.

Similarly, body and soul are soothed when activity is framed by pauses. Stillness and non-doing interludes allow our nervous systems to relax and come into natural balance and harmony.

If our activities are lined up belly to belly, one on top of the other, we must race through them like an athlete running the hurdles in a track and field competition: Jump, sprint, jump, sprint, jump... In contrast, having time and space—even a small amount, as long as it is allotted consciously— around activities invites us to savor, absorb, and actually experience them. Indigenous wisdom teaches that resting and intermittent pauses allow your spirit to catch up with your body.

While there are a few women who seem to thrive in overdrive, the majority of us run the risk of depleting our immune systems, draining our emotional reserves, and fraying our nerves if we run too fast for too long. Too much input and output can make us go kaput.

Does your life have white space? If not, how might you begin to surround your activities with space? Where would you like to pause?

PRACTICE...

- Under-schedule one day this week. If that is too difficult, consciously under-schedule one hour in the next two days.

- Take pleasure in the white space you create.

THROUGHOUT YOUR DAY...

- Surround several activities with mini spaces. For instance, concentrate on taking a few deep breaths while waiting for a Zoom meeting to begin. Look at the trees and grass while waiting for your kids to get ready for an appointment. Take a few minutes after lunch to simply be.

Space highlights that which it surrounds.

FEEDING BODY & SOUL

We all know food is necessary fuel for keeping us alive, alert, and healthy. From experience, many of us also know that the idea of food carries a lot of baggage. The "Hollywoodizing" of body norms, underlying beliefs about our own weight and attractiveness, and how much comfort we get from eating can combine to create a love/hate relationship with food: Too much food, guilt; too little food, guilt. If we eat the wrong kind of food, we get yummy taste, but laced with guilt and lack of wellness; or if we choose good food, change of taste and worry over extra expense. I could go on and on, and I imagine you could also.

Mindfulness, I'm told, can bring you into a whole new relationship with food and eating—which is good news to me because I love to eat. Eating is a complete pleasure for me. I shake my head in wonder—and reach for chocolate—when someone says they can take it or leave it and really eat only to stay alive. Say what?! As you can imagine, weight has been an ongoing dance for me. With effort, exercise, and lots of self-control— not a virtue at which I excel—I can usually keep myself within shouting distance of an appropriate weight. However, with the addition of a couple of pandemic pounds and in the interest of self-acceptance, I'm in the process of expanding my definition of appropriate.

I've also given up guilt and am working on mindful eating to help change old habits, enjoy different foods, and eat more healthfully. Want to join me? Even though I've been thinking, writing, and dreaming about mindfulness for months, I haven't been eating with it until a few short days ago. No, my weight hasn't changed yet. Nor do I feel more energized or bouncy. What has changed, though, is that I am much more aware of my body and how it responds to what I feed it. Plus, I'm also treating it more gently and kindly.

The following practice is what I'm doing to encourage myself to eat mindfully. You will undoubtedly have your own way of doing it. Please

listen to the information your wondrous and unique body gives you and follow
its wisdom.

PRACTICE...

- Consciously choose what you will eat, rather than grabbing the first easy thing.

- Pay attention to each bite. Imagine the food's long journey toward your enjoyment of it.

- Feel gratitude for the food in front of you.

- Notice how the food you eat affects your body.

THROUGHOUT YOUR DAY...

- Acknowledge each mindful food choice you make.

Mindfully eaten food befriends both body and soul.

BLESSINGS OF BREATHING

Breathing is the best medicine. Not only does it keep us alive, it can also interrupt negative thought patterns, bring new vitality to needy body parts, encourage deep sleep, calm jittery nerves, and infuse the brain with energy and power.

Blessing with breath is as simple as it is effective.

Paying Attention to Breath.

Become aware of your breath. Notice breath entering and leaving your nostrils for two or three cycles.

Deepening Breath.

Gently deepen your breath. Feel the difference between shallow and deep breathing. Sense the expansion of your body on the in-breath and enjoy the relaxation of the out-breath.

Directing Breath to Bestow Blessings.

You can direct your breath to anyone or anything. If a friend is having a difficult time, bless them as you breathe out. Something as simple as "Bless you" or "Peace to your heart" is great. Words are not even necessary. Consciously intending to bless another with breath is good enough.

I find it comforting to bless myself with breath if I'm nervous, worried, grieving, or upset in any way. Paying attention to my breath, I might ask that God's blessings flow into me as I inhale and that anything I need to release flows out as I exhale. Inhaling the positive and then exhaling the troublesome usually has a calming influence on me.

If someone's actions or attitudes bother me and I allow irritation and negative thoughts to chafe my psyche, I can often interrupt that self-sabotaging behavior by exhaling a blessing toward the person with whom I am annoyed. Choosing to bless rather than holding onto irritation and annoyance is a blessing in itself. Sending blessings calms the mind, soothes the heart, and helps break the habit of letting irritation or annoyance obscure our joy.

PRACTICE...

- Use a few breaths each morning to consciously invite blessings into your body, heart, mind, and emotions.

- When you think of someone you love, send them two or three breath blessings.

- If you become upset with someone, breathe blessings toward them.

- Breathe love and acceptance into yourself and breathe out goodwill to others.

Breath is an original blessing.

KEEPING HOPE AFLOAT

Hope is an inside job. Although poet Alexander Pope said, "Hope springs eternal in the human breast," hope springs faster and more consistently when we consciously encourage and consistently practice keeping hope afloat in our hearts and souls.

A word of caution: As I write this, we are living in unprecedented times, with the Covid-19 pandemic, racial injustice now rightfully front and center, epic uncertainty, and disheartening divisiveness. Everything "normal" is up for grabs. In order to keep hope alive, it's extremely important to monitor what we allow ourselves to see, hear, and feel, especially in regard to the media. Yes, we need to know what's going on. Yes, much of it will break our hearts wide open, and I believe that is, hopefully, one of the gifts of the current challenges. We need to care and change, personally and societally. But, very importantly, we also need to gently take care of ourselves throughout the process. This is not easily done, but it's crucial to do.

Because your subconscious mind accepts as real both your personal experiences but also those you watch or imagine vividly, one of the best ways to take care of yourself is to mindfully and wisely choose what you watch and read.

Images imprint deeply. The disturbing pictures and commentary favored by the media can act as emotional acid, etching the pain and suffering we witness into our psyches. Such images can pull the plug on our reserves of hope. Limiting your exposure to sensationalism of all kinds is wise. Allow yourself to be as informed as you feel the need to be but not deformed by overexposure and overstimulation.

Hope is the proverbial light at the end of any dark tunnel. Hope is the ballast that keeps you moving forward and helps you continue to believe in beauty, love, and survival even when personal and public waters are turbulent. With hope, it is possible to keep your head above water while navigating stormy seas. Hope can also make everyday life much brighter, more joyous, and more doable.

Ashley, an RN in my neighborhood, is a great example of nurturing hope in hard times. During the inevitable dark times of hospitalization for Covid-19, she consciously courted hope. Allowing people to help and praying were two of her important hope-boosters. Ashley also intentionally chose to be a student of Covid rather than its victim, and as such, she kept asking herself insightful questions such as, "What lessons am I learning here?" and "How can this make me a better nurse?" Although she's not back to work yet, Ashley believes she'll be more understanding and present to patients after her experiences because at a visceral level, she knows what it's like to be one.

PRACTICE...

- Make a commitment to keeping hope afloat in your heart and soul.

- If you find yourself in the dark, search out a pinprick, flash, or ray of light right here, right now.

- Intentionally look on the bright side.

- Three times a day, take a moment to find a spark of hope in nature, in your own life, at your home, or in the world.

Hope is contagious. Please spread it.

INFUSING MEANING INTO THE MONOTONOUS

Maybe because I needed something tangible to push against at the beginning of the Covid-19 pandemic, incessant handwashing irritated the hell out of me. Each time I grudgingly scrubbed away, I also grumped away feeling impatient and petulant. Handwashing was helpful for germ removal but certainly not great for my emotional, mental, and spiritual well-being.

During one grouchy handwashing session, mindsight kicked in and I saw how many times a day resistant self-talk was tarnishing my attitude. As always, awareness was the key to change, and I knew I wanted to infuse some sort of meaning into the monotonous task of handwashing. I tried singing as I slowly counted to twenty seconds but found that neither meaningful nor fun. Watching bubbles form the longer I scrubbed was a bit intriguing to the art lover part of me but still didn't have the soothing balm of meaning I was yearning for.

When a friend shared that she chanted a mantra while washing her hands, my heart resonated with the idea. A mantra is a motivating chant or song used to help concentration during meditation, or to calm and encourage both mind and heart at any time. My favorite Buddhist mantra has long been Om Mani Padme Hum. Of the many meanings I've read for this specific chant, I prefer "Let every word, deed, and thought be motivated by love and compassion for all beings." Augmented by conscious gratitude and appreciation for my hands, singing this chant extolling love and compassion is now the centerpiece of my handwashing intervals. By infusing meaning into it, handwashing has become a sweet and thoughtful mindfulness practice that I actually look forward to.

Life is punctuated with monotonous and tedious times and activities. We do ourselves a compassionate and calming favor by infusing them with meaning.

PRACTICE...

- Become aware of one or two ho-hum tasks or activities that you tend to ignore or resist.

THROUGHOUT YOUR DAY...

- Get creative about instilling a little pizzazz and meaning into at least one of the tasks or activities you noticed.

With mindful intention, almost everything can be infused with meaning.

REBELLING WITH RADICAL WISDOM

In our fast-paced, future-obsessed society, aspiring to fully inhabit each moment is radically wise—and is actually a subtle form of rebellion against the less-than-mindful status quo.

I don't know about you, but as a long-term nice girl, a bit of rebellion appeals to me. Mindfulness as rebellion…I like it! If you and I start a mindfulness uprising within our own lives, who knows where it might lead? While living an increasingly mindful life, could we, either personally or globally, condone war? Could we allow children to starve or be needlessly separated from their parents? Could we remain quiet in the face of injustice and inequality? Could we take those we love for granted? Actively engaged in the radical wisdom of mindfully living in the present moment, could we treat ourselves unkindly? I doubt it.

We women are wonderfully powerful and wise, plus more influential than we dare to imagine. Which, of course, means that you are powerfully wise and influential. As with all worthwhile endeavors, being aware of and accepting your own radical wisdom begins internally. Paying attention to the wisdom, grace, and courage you express each moment provides a treasure trove of insight into your own incredible qualities and gives you the audacity to rebel in conscious, peaceful ways.

With mindfulness, even difficult times can be incredibly revealing and enlightening. They help us to know ourselves better, appreciate our strength and wisdom more deeply, and increase our capacity for compassion.

The current moment is your home, your solace, the only place and time where you can find balance, happiness, and empowerment. Settling into each moment as it really is—not as you wish it were—allows you to appreciate your life in all its sadness and glory.

PRACTICE...

- Sit quietly for a few breaths and simply pay attention to the moment, no matter what it holds or how it feels.

- Jot down three ways in which you are wise right now. (It isn't necessary for you to be acting on the wisdom.)

- At least once a day, ask for guidance in using your wisdom. Breathe in guidance, breathe out resistance to your own power and influence.

THROUGHOUT YOUR DAY...

- Several times, breathe out the affirmation, "My wisdom blesses me and the world." You don't have to believe the statement, simply make a commitment to repeating it with as much feeling as possible and miracles can happen.

Radical wisdom

Blooms when powerful women

Practice mindfulness.

Savoring the Qualities of a Quiet Mind

"We need to be quiet. We need to be happy. We need to be still. God's holy peace is all around me. When I am still, it is reflected within me."

—Hugh Prather

I've chuckled with friends who, like me, are trying to live mindfully, and told them we might make better progress if we started a new twelve-step program called SAA: Stimulation Addicts Anonymous. There certainly have been times in my life when I could have benefited from meeting with a supportive group and admitting my addiction to the emotional roller coaster of drama, trauma, and constant activity. As a young woman, I was lucky enough to have my own personal SAA sponsor in the form of Annabelle Woodard, my spiritual mother and mentor. Annabelle gently showed me I was a stimulation junkie. "Your mind is always in turmoil, Sue, and your life is like a roller coaster, soaring to very high highs and crashing to equally low lows." I, of course, dramatically denied it...at the time. She was right, of course.

Although I now see myself as a recovering drama queen, it still takes consistent awareness to avoid being sucked into the stimulation vortex to which our society as a whole seems addicted. For me and many other stimulation addicts, mindfulness is a wonderful form of rehab. Being mindful helps free us from the habitual firestorms of mental and emotional chaos, over-busyness, and the debilitating habits of anxiety, worry, and guilt.

In this chapter, I have chosen to highlight a few of the qualities inherent in a quiet mind. The qualities we'll be working with are: Clarity, Equanimity, Choice, Tolerance, Optimism, Wisdom, Awe, Receptivity, and Spaciousness. The practice of these qualities can help you be happy and still, and hopefully even reflect the peace of God to our beleaguered and divided but nonetheless beautiful world and her inhabitants.

SEEING WITH CLARITY

Feelings of confusion, ambiguity, and murkiness are incredibly uncomfortable. In the throes of such feelings, we want to move ahead but don't have a clue which direction to turn. We long for the relief of making a good decision but can't decide which is the right one. We want to make a choice, but each has both pros and cons, and we simply can't bring ourselves to say, "That's the one!"

If this sounds familiar to you, what can you do?

Nothing…wait, nothing!?

Yep, nothing.

Many years ago, Elisabeth Kübler-Ross, MD, the eminent psychiatrist who brought the subjects of death, dying, and grief out in the open, introduced me to a little book entitled The Quiet Mind, saying it was the only thing that helped her quiet her own mind. If Elisabeth, a dynamo of constant energy, was helped by this book, I had to have it. The Quiet Mind is a collection of short paragraphs by White Eagle, a spiritual teacher. My favorite passage— one I often turn to when opening the book at random—is, "If you do not know what to do, do nothing." White Eagle goes on to say we need to still our minds and not act from confusion. He believes that clarity and right action can best surface from the depths of a quiet, serene mind. I have found this to be true.

Of course, the mindful approach to doing nothing when feeling unclear is not really doing nothing. To gain clarity, you breathe. You wait. You ask for clarity. You sit quietly and consciously invite your mind to settle. You visualize clarity. You accept yourself just as you are right in this murky moment, trusting that clarity will come. And you turn your awareness to the ebb and flow of the current moment. Returning to the here and now interrupts the mental wheel spinning that inevitably accompanies confusion and doubt.

PRACTICE...

- Without judgment, notice when you feel unclear or confused and resist the impulse to act from uncertainty.

- Sit quietly with your eyes closed for a few minutes and concentrate as fully as possible on the inflow and outgo of your completely reliable breath.

- For the next several breaths (at least seven, please), silently affirm "I know that I know" as you inhale and "Thank you" as you exhale.

THROUGHOUT YOUR DAY...

- Sing snatches of uplifting songs, such as India Arie's I Am Light or an oldie like Johnny Nash's I Can See Clearly Now.

- Repeat "I know that I know" or "I trust that I know" whenever you remember to or whenever you begin to feel anxious.

You do know.

EXPERIENCING EQUANIMITY

When you think of the word "equanimity," you may think of things like mental or emotional composure and stability in all circumstances, steadiness of mind under stress or tension, or calmness and equilibrium. A few of my own definitions are letting go of how we think things should be, radical acceptance, and not getting our knickers in too tight a knot over anything, especially that which we can't control.

Being a lover of words, the word equanimity appeals to me. 'Equanimity' has a wonderful flowing sound that brings to mind an unhurried mountain stream leisurely making its way toward reunion with its source. Nothing deters or disturbs such a stream. Faced with obstacles, it does not resist or give up resentfully but rather resolutely and peacefully finds a way to continue its journey.

Many women, myself included, do not come into this life as naturally even-tempered, accepting, free-flowing people able to remain calm and peaceful no matter what the circumstances. Some of us feel more like storm-tossed seas than tranquil streams. Lori, my dental hygienist, was a turbulent sea. "I used to lock and load on the differences between myself and others and allow that to irritate and nag at me and separate me from them," she explained. "But I'm a totally different person now. Even though there's been no change in my circumstances, there's been a huge change in my attitudes, responses, and feelings. And my blood pressure's a lot lower."

How did Lori make the transformation? By practicing meditation and mindfulness. Although Lori meditates at least forty minutes a day and sometimes for as long as three hours at a time, she stresses that consistency is more important than time. I hope she's right, because most of us will not meditate for hours on end and all of us will lapse in and out of mindfulness regularly. Fortunately, we can always invite equanimity back into our lives and selves by consistently returning to mindfulness and gifting ourselves with quiet times.

PRACTICE...

- Accept yourself just as you are right now, whether wild and stormy or calm and peaceful.

- Set an intention to quiet your mind and move toward equanimity.

- With your eyes lightly closed, imagine your breath as gentle undulations of cool, tranquil water. Allow yourself to be soothed by the soft, sweet movement.

THROUGHOUT YOUR DAY...

- Consciously ride the gentle waves of your breath for a few moments at least two or three times. This may also be a good way to lull yourself to sleep.

Breathe yourself calm and composed.

MAKING THE BEST CHOICE

Choice is freedom. As with most freedoms, choice carries tremendous responsibility. We want to make choices that resonate with our heart's desires and keep us going in the right direction. In addition, as women, we are usually very cognizant of making choices that are also good for those we love.

Each day you have many opportunities to state a preference, mull over options, and choose between alternatives. The majority of the time, choices are simple. Cereal or eggs? Jeans or tights? Other choices are life-altering. Have children or not? Take this job or that one? Surgery, chemotherapy, or holistic treatment?

Simple choices are easy and often made by rote. Difficult choices, however, are best made from the clarity of a quiet mind.

After being diagnosed with cancer, my dear friend Kate was faced with a barrage of choices. Naturally, she wanted to make those that gave her the best chance of recovery as well as those likely to bring a modicum of solace to her husband, sons, and large extended family. Although Kate was an exceptionally clear headed and independent woman, she understandably experienced some confusion while sorting and culling her options, managing her own feelings, and being considerate of others' feelings as well.

In answer to my query about how she had decided which treatments to pursue, Kate answered, "Finally, I simply had to tell everyone—family and doctors included—to leave me alone for a while. I needed solitude to uncover what I really thought and felt." She returned from a silent weekend retreat, "knowing in my heart what I needed to do." By separating herself from the cacophony of other people's feelings and well-meaning advice, Kate was able to quiet her mind, tune in to her heart, and choose treatments that felt right to her.

Each time I visited Kate during and after treatments, we followed a little ritual. First, I asked her how her body was, and she would give me as much of an update as she wanted to share. Next, I asked how her heart was. Without fail, her answer was, "My heart is good. My heart is always good." Even though the outcome was not the one for which we hoped and prayed, Kate's peace of mind never faltered; I'm sure in part because she had quieted her mind enough to follow her heart.

PRACTICE...

- When faced with serious decisions, be very mindful of the scared, angry, or hurt part of yourself and nurture her in ways that feel good. Be loving rather than judgmental toward yourself.

- Take time for solitude. Breathe in serenity and peace. Breathe out anxiety and confusion.

- Gently, but deeply, breathe into your heart, asking it to help you make the right decision.

THROUGHOUT YOUR DAY...

- Bring your awareness to your heart and breathe peace, calm, and quiet into it. If it feels helpful, put your hands over your heart while you breathe.

A quiet mind allows you to choose from your heart.

UPPING TOLERANCE LEVELS

We will be exploring two kinds of tolerance in this practice: tolerance for living beings and tolerance for circumstances. Tolerance for living beings, ourselves included, consists of an attitude of acceptance and fairness coupled with genuine respect. Tolerance for circumstances concerns our ability to tolerate unfavorable conditions that run the gamut from slightly irritating to totally disastrous.

So what does a quiet mind have to do with tolerance levels? Quite a bit. If your mind is in flea-on-a-hot-griddle mode, it will automatically revert to habitual beliefs, feelings, and actions in order to hurry on to the next thing. A quiet mind, on the other hand, is aware of alternatives and has the freedom to choose among them. A very small example happened to me the other day. I was driving to my grandson's baseball game and a young man in a truck kept riding my bumper. Before practicing mindfulness, tailgating was one of my favorite intolerable annoyances. Well, truth be told, I was pretty annoyed this time for a few minutes also, until I remembered to quiet my mind.

A quiet mind can return us to the moment and wake us up to what is really happening now. Is the driver kissing my tailpipe really making my drive intolerable? No. Is he a selfish, thoughtless, chauvinist clod who shouldn't be allowed on the road? Probably not. By now I was smiling and gently chiding myself about how easily I regressed to old thoughts and how quickly I became upset as a result of them.

It felt so good to remember the situation could be seen and experienced differently. For fun, I created a new story, one in which the inconsiderate man became a dedicated husband and father rushing to be with his family for some important reason. Given my new tolerance of Mr. Tailgater, I actually felt like sending him a little blessing rather than the original gesture I'd wanted to make.

A quiet mind is a peaceful mind. From the steady calm of a quiet mind, you have the ability to remember that tolerance is more easily practiced when you are present in the current moment.

PRACTICE...

PRACTICE...

- When you feel intolerant or upset, bring your attention to the current moment. Feel your feet on the floor and be aware of your breath.

- If you notice a negative mind-movie running in your head, have a little fun by changing it to a positive drama or comedy.

- Send a brief blessing to sources of irritation or intolerance.

THROUGHOUT YOUR DAY...

- Become aware of your feet and the surface upon which they rest.

Tolerance is a kissin' cousin of compassion.

CULTIVATING COCKEYED OPTIMISM

Most of us know at least a little bit about the black holes wandering around our galaxy. We know, for instance, that a black hole will voraciously gobble up any star, planet, or cosmic debris in its path. Pessimism is a lot like a personal black hole. Left unchecked, pessimism darkens your attitude, swallows your hope, and effectively squelches any enthusiasm you may otherwise feel for circumstances, experiences, or other people.

Studies show optimists live longer, heal faster, have more friends, and enjoy life more than pessimists. Given such good reasons to cultivate optimism, why do we occasionally find ourselves slumping through our days like Eeyore lamenting the inadequacies of his tail? One reason is that pessimism is easier than optimism. Simply reading or watching the news and consistently paying attention to pessimistic people around us can be enough to suck us into the black hole of gloom and doom.

In reality, the least productive thing you can do both personally and globally is to allow your days to be devoured by black-hole pessimism. Concentrating on worst-case scenarios permits pessimism to become your psyche's default setting. Consistent pessimism also hinders your ability to find positive outcomes to problems that need solving.

On the other hand, because optimists look on the bright side of events and conditions and expect favorable outcomes in most situations, they have the energy and enthusiasm to do their part in making sure tomorrow will be better than today. Optimism fuels forward movement and hope. Cultivating optimism gives you the ability to be happier and healthier in the present while also shaping a more positive future for yourself and your loved ones. Optimists get things done. Fabulous work, beautiful babies, cures for disease, and great relationships, as well as most other worthwhile endeavors are usually fueled by cockeyed optimism. An attitude of "I think I can... I think I can..." proves true more often than not.

PRACTICE...

- Gently, but with great commitment, change pessimistic thoughts to optimistic ones. (Believing the thoughts is not necessary for this practice to work.)

- As much as possible, associate with upbeat people.

THROUGHOUT YOUR DAY...

- Notice at least two or three examples of optimism: a small ant moving a large crumb, a toddler getting up from a fall to try walking again, a plant growing out of a rock crevasse, an old couple holding hands...

An optimist isn't always happy,
but she believes she will be soon.

TUNING IN TO WISDOM

Wisdom is not book learning, but rather a quality or state of knowing what is true or right coupled with the judgment to discern constructive action. Wisdom is the insight and intuition contained in the proverbial still, small voice that only a quiet mind can hear and know. I love the way Unity minister Nat Carter describes the voice within: "The still, small voice within us is polite. It waits for space to be heard, not raising its volume or interrupting to get our attention." Darn! There are definitely times when I'd prefer my inner wisdom to cut through all the mind chatter, speak in a loud, large voice, and grab me by the ears, saying, "Listen up, Sue!" But very rarely is it so forceful.

To encourage the still, small voice to speak, I begin each writing session with a simple practice in which I call in my guardian angels, muses, and any other helper beings who want to be a part of the circle. The components of the practice are straightforward: the invitation, a prayer about opening myself to my own and angelic wisdom and intuition, and a thank you for being present. Sometimes I feel little tingles that announce the presence of my angels and helper beings to me. Often, physical assurances are lacking and I must simply trust they have answered my request. Because writing is such a solitary endeavor, it's a comfort to believe I'm accompanied by helpers from a higher realm.

On days when writing is laborious and my mind and heart feel as if they are unsuccessfully trying to surface from a vat of gelatin, it's often because I've forgotten the practice. Not being as fluent and creative as I desire alerts me to the fact that quieting down before writing, taking time to ask for help, and then giving thanks for it are tried and true ways for me to be better attuned to the still, small voice of wisdom.

The voice of wisdom is inherent within us and willing to guide us when we stop to listen. Of course, there are going to be times when we feel we've been

silent as stone, and the still, small voice is still too quiet to hear. During
those times, the challenge is to continue quieting your mind anyway by
stopping and asking, quieting and listening, trusting and waiting. Waiting is
difficult but worth the effort because a quiet, uncluttered mind is a natural
antenna for whispers of wisdom from within.

PRACTICE...

· Take a few cleansing and quieting breaths. Even if you don't hear or
sense it, give thanks for the still, small voice of wisdom within.

· As you continue to breath softly, use your in-breath to say, "I open
to..." and your out-breath to say, "my unique wisdom within."

THROUGHOUT YOUR DAY...

· Affirm that the still, small voice of wisdom is alive within you. A quiet
mind hears whispers of wisdom.

Wisdom whispers within.

ACTIVATING AWE

Cathy, a wonderful young woman I know, approached me at church and
enthusiastically asked, "Have you ever been to Hawaii?" Since I lived there
for five years early in my marriage, the answer was affirmative. "Omigosh,
it was beautiful!" she raved. "My awe-o-meter was off the charts while I
was there!"

I loved Cathy's reference to her awe-o-meter. And I was struck by the
fact that I hadn't been awed in a while. Did that mean awesome things
had disappeared from my life? No. What it did mean was that I'd gotten
too caught up in distractions and mind-mucking to recognize anything

as awe-inspiring. Cathy's comments made me aware that I hadn't been paying attention to the beauty around me lately. To help bring myself back to mindfully registering the wonder and reverence of the world, I took my little dog Lily for an awe-o-meter walk that afternoon.

Lily was a great companion for such a walk because her aroma-awe of each and every smell along the way gave me plenty of time to open my eyes, quiet my mind, and actually see and appreciate what was present. Even though Mother Nature was in winter mode during our walk, there was much to inspire awe. The resident blue heron showed herself, a muskrat swam among some ducks, and Lily herself made me smile and feel incredibly grateful for the love this little ragamuffin brings to my own and Gene's lives. I saw more on that conscious awe-o-meter walk than I had on many, many previous ones.

J. Krishnamurti says "To understand the immeasurable, the mind must be extraordinarily quiet, still." Naturally, none of us is going to have a quiet mind all of the time. Nor should we even expect that of ourselves. However, we can choose minutes in which to be quietly and consciously mindful of experiences, people, ideas, and loveliness that bring a sense of awe and reverence to our hearts. Being mindful and really seeing the immeasurable beauty and wonder in our own neighborhoods can be awesome in its own right. We don't have to go to Hawaii to have our awe-o-meters rocket off the charts.

PRACTICE...

- Choose to walk somewhere you normally drive. Consciously look at and register the beauty you see.

- Take a tour of one of the rooms in your home. Become aware of your precious objects. Remember their significance. Touch the surfaces of furniture and memorabilia, feel the textures, allow your hands and eyes to caress and admire them. Awesome, right?

- Activate your awe-o-meter at least twice a day.

A few mindful moments can make an awesome difference.

SAYING *YES* TO RECEPTIVITY

If you've ever thought of someone and they call soon after, or if you are thinking about a topic and the person you're with begins talking about the same subject, you've experienced what I call energy arcs between people. We are more receptive to the arcs of energy between ourselves and others when our minds are quiet and free from static. A quiet mind gives us the readiness to receive impressions or ideas from others, our own higher selves, and the universe. We, however, need to supply the willingness to receive and register intuitive nudges, wisdom whispers, and creative urges.

A quiet, receptive mind is a friendly mind, interested in and aware of nuances within ourselves and others that a cluttered mind doesn't have the time or inclination to notice. Openness and accessibility are also qualities of a quiet mind. We are drawn to people who are interested in us and open with us—people whose ideas and emotions are accessible and readily expressed. In other words, women love to truly and genuinely connect with others. One reason we value our women friends so much is that they also want to make meaningful connections and are usually good at it.

Many years ago, both of my sons were seriously injured within days of each other. The boys' injuries were dream-shattering for them, and consequently, for me also. After days of emotional turmoil, my husband and I capped off the trauma by having a big fight. Stunned from one too many blows, I fled the house to seek solace from my dear friend Bonnie. Even though I hadn't taken the time to call, I desperately hoped she'd be home. She was, and she provided the consolation I needed. Later, she told me that she'd had plans but felt me coming and so she stayed home to meet me. Bonnie was receptive to the energy arc between us; consequently, she was available when I desperately needed her.

Not only does being receptive to help make us better friends and lovers, it also gives us a clearer conduit to the realms of the Divine. I believe many forms of help and inspiration hover around us waiting to be called upon. Maybe the energy arc between Bonnie and myself was really an angel tapping her on the shoulder. No matter what our individual beliefs, help, inspiration, and intuition do come into our minds. Our task is to say 'yes' to receptivity by quieting our minds.

PRACTICE...

- Set the intention to be aware of energy arcs between you and those you love.

- When intuition speaks, listen. When inspiration strikes, act.

THROUGHOUT YOUR DAY...

- Take a moment to breathe in quietness and invite receptivity.

The quieter you become, the more you can hear.

—Ram Dass

OPENING TO SPACIOUSNESS

As Lao-tzu, the Chinese philosopher who is known as the father of Taoism, assures us, "To the mind that is still, the whole universe surrenders." The idea of the whole universe surrendering to me is a bit too daunting, so my interpretation of Lao-tzu's message is that living with a quiet mind promises life and love will flow more smoothly.

Stillness is an ever-present theme in mindfulness and meditation teachings—the core around which they circle. Meditation teachers advise that the stillness of meditation creates spaciousness, a roominess in which the mind can rest and find relief from the stories we tell ourselves about ourselves, our lives, and the obligations and responsibilities we carry. In my own practice, I've come to think of meditation as an oasis of stillness in the midst of everyday life. It is a sacred place where I find sanctuary from both the joy and sadness most days offer, a retreat in which there is nothing to do and no one to please, a space for simply being, and a place to fall back in love with myself.

Because I find meditation such an oasis, you'd think I'd be disciplined enough to do it every day, but I'm sorry to say I'm not. I usually practice mindfulness each day, but often mindful moments are wedged in between activities or sleep cycles. And there are days when my mind is too full or too uneasy to be truly mindful. I'm learning to see these undisciplined, overfull, and worried times as part of my practice also—an opportunity to be gentle with myself even though I'm not being a good mindfulness meditation practitioner, or a good anything. Please don't be hard on yourself if you, too, wander away from your chosen path. Your ongoing task is to love yourself through all of life's detours.

In fact, being still enough to create the openness and generosity of heart to love yourself in the moment is the greatest gift spaciousness has to offer. When you genuinely love and accept yourself, love naturally flows freely from you to all other beings and it does indeed feel as if the whole universe is surrendering to you.

PRACTICE...

- Sit still for a minute or two with no focus or agenda.

- Gently bring your attention to your breath, allowing it to rise and fall naturally.

- With each breath cycle, imagine yourself effortlessly expanding into spaciousness.

- Name the spaciousness "Love," and rest within it.

THROUGHOUT YOUR DAY...

- Imagine, and if possible, feel yourself at peace in a space of love.

Flowing steadily

From a spacious quiet mind,

Peace, love, harmony.

Chapter 5

Accepting What Is

"Mindfulness is simply being aware of what is happening right now without wishing it were different; enjoying the pleasant without holding on when it changes (which it will), being with the unpleasant without fearing it will always be this way (which it won't)."

—James Baraz

In a society that stresses being in control, self-
reliance, and the belief that we create our own reality, the concept of
mindful acceptance is a hard one to get our arms around. While I definitely
have faith in the ideas of self-reliance and creating our own reality, I
also believe that gracious acceptance of circumstances, emotions, and
experiences is very often a necessary, though neglected, part of life's process.

For many years, I was much better at resisting and attempting to control
realities I didn't like than I was at gracefully accepting them. Although
familiar with the adage "Go with the flow," I was an against-the-current
swimmer. Eventually, it became apparent that 'Resistance is futile,' as Star
Trek's Borg like to expound. For me, resistance magnified any pain I was
feeling and locked me in the embrace of that which I resisted.

Before I could relax my grip on the fantasy that I might control anything
other than my own thoughts, attitudes, and choices, I needed to stop
equating acceptance with capitulation, victimization, and helplessness. With
practice, it ultimately became apparent that acceptance actually helped me
feel self-reliant and able to co-create my reality with God. Surprisingly, I
discovered that acceptance is empowering, whereas resistance is enervating.
Of course, resistance and a desire to control can still be my knee-jerk
reactions to some stimuli, but still, more often than not, I can now start
moving toward acceptance as soon as I become aware I've regressed to my
old tightfisted, tight-hearted, uptight behavioral pattern.

EARNING ANGEL WINGS

During a brief hospital stay last year, I met a young male nurse who was a
model of gracious acceptance. Dale and I made a sweet connection during
our middle-of-the-night conversations, and he was definitely one of the
silver linings in the whole experience. A brief story of his life unfolded as he
took time to chat with me while taking care of nursing business. His story
is bittersweet.

Dale was a second-year medical student when his wife was severely injured in an automobile accident. She survived the crash but was left with serious mental and physical challenges. Even if they'd had the money for him to stay in school, he said he would have dropped out because, "Our vows said for better or worse. We're a team. She'd do it for me. No big thing." He went on to explain he worked at night so he could be with his wife during the day, "You know, for company and to take her to doctor appointments and therapy sessions."

I was struck by how happy Dale was, so okay with and accepting of the dramatic turn his life had taken. To me, this man has earned his angel wings.

Dale's response to tragedy was so benevolent that I'm concerned your gut reaction might be, "I couldn't possibly react in such a loving way," as mine was. In reality, we don't know how we will act and react until faced with specific experiences. Maybe you and I would also be angelic if placed in Dale's shoes.

Once again, your task is to love and accept yourself whether you are mindfully and graciously accepting all that comes your way or miserably resisting each and every experience and feeling. I know I harp on the need for self-love, but it's because self-love is absolutely the bedrock of your life journey. With a foundation of acceptance, respect, and love for yourself, you have the stability, security, and courage to set about earning your angel wings in all areas of life.

PRACTICE...

- If acceptance is particularly difficult for you, please treat yourself gently and start small.

- Choose one insignificant challenge to be accepting of—a slow checkout line, dirty socks on the floor, a computer glitch, and so on.

- Be aware of your body as you experience resistance, breathe into the areas that are tense, and encourage yourself to relax into acceptance.

THROUGHOUT YOUR DAY...

- Notice resistance and consciously choose acceptance in its place. Because it usually takes a while for feelings to match intentions, please be patient with yourself.

Angel wings are earned one tiny feather at a time.

GIVING UP GRUMBLING

As a therapist, I believe a certain amount of catharsis is necessary for our mental and physical well-being. Built-up energy must be expelled in useful ways or it has a tendency to turn inward and sour into illness, fear, or any number of destructive beliefs and expectations. That said, I also know that consistent complaining can be unhealthy, habit-forming, and personality deforming. Grumbling and complaining erode your happiness as well as your ability to feel goodwill toward others. Grumbling births grouches. Grouches are hard to be around and not usually popular with themselves or anyone else.

As an antidote to the self-defeating habit of grumbling, Will Bowen, a minister in Kansas City, Missouri, challenges his congregation—and the world—to stop complaining, criticizing, gossiping, and using sarcasm for twenty-one days straight in order to break the habit. "Complaining draws all of its essence from negativity," he explains. "When you complain, you typically do it to attract attention or sympathy. You're sending out this vibrational energy that you're a victim, and the universe responds with more negativity."

To help effect positive change, Rev. Bowen and his congregation provide purple bracelets to people who feel they could benefit from a reminder as they change a negative habit to a positive one. Wearers are to switch the bracelet from one hand to the other when they find themselves complaining, gossiping, criticizing, or using sarcasm, and after the switch—this is the hard part—start their twenty-one-day cycle over. At the end of an email the other day, a friend wrote, with a smiley face, "I've changed my band fourteen times during this one email." Since he is definitely not a chronic complainer, I see both his humor and his email as a constructive way to release a little pent-up energy.

Complaint-filled grumbling and acceptance rarely coexist.

PRACTICE...

- Without judgment, notice when you complain and thank yourself for being aware.

- Mindfully and gently decide if it's good for you to continue thinking or speaking as you are or if it would be better to change your thoughts and words. Act accordingly.

- At the end of the day, review each time you consciously gave up grumbling.

THROUGHOUT YOUR DAY...

- Transform grumbling with acceptance.

Giving up compulsive complaining is beneficial
to your health and welfare.

CHOOSING THE PARTS YOU PLAY

William Shakespeare assured us that, "All the world's a stage, and all the men and women merely players. They have their exits and their entrances, and one man in his time plays many parts…" Frequently, I think it's healthy and fun to consider life a stage upon which we play out different story lines. While there are some immutable parameters within which your dramas and comedies are acted out—gender, nationality, health, quality of parenting received, and physical appearance, to name a few—it is within your power to choose your response to life's scripts, and in so doing, pick the best aspect of yourself for the current part you need to play.

For years, I had a penchant for miscasting myself as either the heroine tied to the railroad tracks, an underappreciated Cinderella, or Brunhilda-the-Terrible in life's dramas. Choosing stronger, more adult facets of myself to take center stage now keeps both my inner Drama Queen and Victim free from acting on their addiction to the adrenaline of drama.

Does choosing how to act and who to be complement accepting what is? I think so. Acceptance is not allowing yourself to be run over by circumstances; it is often simply nonresistance. Therefore, by becoming aware of the script that has been metaphorically tossed in your lap and saying, "Ah so…here is the playbill for this evening," you are accepting the situation with equanimity. From a place of balance and acceptance, you have the power to choose the character within you that best fits the role you're asked to play in the moment. For instance, if a family member is ill, the best role for the situation might be Tenacious Medical Advocate. When a friend or child is emotionally wounded, your part could be that of Safe, Supportive Shoulder. Ideally, we accept what has come our way and then mindfully and wisely choose to respond from the most appropriate actor available in our internal cast of characters.

PRACTICE...

- Just for fun, think of a current situation in your life and choose a character within you that can handle the scenario beautifully.

- Act the part, being mindful of how it feels to express this aspect of yourself.

- Thank that part of yourself and continue to use the role if it works.

THROUGHOUT YOUR DAY...

- Accept what comes your way and mindfully choose who responds.

- Have fun with it.

You are the star of your production.

WAITING FOR RIPENESS

Allowed to mature naturally, fruits and vegetables ripen in their own time according to the type of soil, sun, and rain they enjoy. Forcing them to grow in accordance with our schedules and desires by placing them in a hothouse seems an apt metaphor for many of the daily demands we place on ourselves. We expect ourselves to become proficient in everything from computers to parenting skills quickly and effortlessly, and we often feel like failures if we don't know what to do right now when faced with a crucial decision. It's as if we expect our own maturation process to resemble the instant access technology we rely on. But it ain't gonna happen.

The sooner we accept the fact that time ripens all things—including human beings—the more calm, patient, and peaceful we will become. Like fruits and vegetables need the sun and rain to come to fruition, we need and deserve to ripen slowly and fully in the light of our own acceptance. Poet

Rainer Maria Rilke encourages us to, "Have patience with everything unresolved in your heart and try to love the questions themselves."

Rilke's statement is an important one for me. Reading it encourages me to relax into the unknown, trusting that ripeness will happen in the fullness of time. It also helps me be okay with uncertainty at times and gives me permission to allow decisions and answers to unfold organically.

As I write about ripeness, the difference between vine-ripened and hothouse tomatoes keeps coming into my mind. I was raised in hot, humid Missouri, where I learned to love garden-fresh tomatoes. But I like them peeled. Not a problem for vine-ripened tomatoes. Their skin slides off easily. However, the best way to get the skin off hothouse tomatoes is to first dunk them in boiling water prior to peeling—but they still don't taste like real tomatoes. Hmmm… How often have I gotten myself in hot water by doing or saying something before the time was ripe? And how many times have I expected myself to be or do something for which I was not yet fully ripened and ready? Quite a few times, actually, and the forced, accelerated results were not as delicious as they might have been had I trusted ripeness would come in due time.

PRACTICE...

- Lovingly become aware of areas in which you might be pushing yourself faster than you can comfortably and competently go.

- Take a few slow, deep breaths, and relax into the idea of ripeness, and allowing it to grow within your heart and soul.

THROUGHOUT YOUR DAY...

- Ask yourself if this idea, decision, action, relationship, or emotion is really fully ripe. If not, wait, trusting that time and intention ripen all things.

The sweetness of a ripe fruit is worth the wait.

MAKING HEAVEN OF HELL

Sorrow, loss, and physical pain are facts of life. Some of us are fortunate enough to experience these only a little, while some of us seem to have far more than our share of each. How we respond to pain and sadness is entirely up to us. John Milton made a wonderful point when he said, "The mind is its own place, and in itself, can make a Heaven of Hell, a Hell of Heaven."

My former client, Patty, was the queen of making a heaven of hell. Patty's husband was killed by friendly fire in a military action leaving her with five children to raise on very little money. On top of that, Patty endured painful bouts of fibromyalgia, and her youngest child had Down's syndrome. She came to see me because, as she said, "I get a little blue sometimes and just wanted an adult to talk to." A little blue! I couldn't even imagine surviving under such conditions. But survive Patty did, along with all her kids. I was struck by the fact that Patty made at least a passing reference to how lucky she was in each of our sessions. It was no mystery who was inspiring whom in our meetings.

Patty made me wonder why some people seem to stumble into little potholes when faced with pain, loss, or sadness whereas others plummet into the deepest craters. Working with other clients who tended to fall into hellish craters helped me understand a few of the differences between those who potholed and those who cratered. Here are some examples:

Pothole Stumblers	Crater Crashers
Concentrate on staying in the here and now	Worry about the future
Consciously work on accepting what is	Believe things shouldn't be as they are
See themselves as survivors	View themselves as victims
Try to have positive thoughts	Are plagued by fearful thoughts

The quality of our thoughts and beliefs about ourselves can create both heaven and hell.

PRACTICE...

- When fearful thoughts invade your mind, bring yourself into the safety of the here and now by concentrating on each breath.

- As often as necessary, remind yourself of your innate strength and resilience.

THROUGHOUT YOUR DAY...

- Find small ways to feel lucky.

Heaven or hell; we can choose.

REMEMBERING TO EXHALE

I once went on a roller coaster in Las Vegas that I'm sure was designed by a demented Dr. Frankenstein type for the sole purpose of supporting local chiropractors. Its twists and turns, jerks and lunges, were more than any human body could comfortably withstand. Except for screaming, I held my breath throughout the entire battering. In pain and dripping with adrenaline, I finally staggered off. After taking one look at me, my definitely smarter, non-riding spouse said anxiously, "Breathe, Susie!" As I huffed out the breath I'd been holding, my body began releasing accumulated tension through uncontrollable trembling.

Life is sometimes like that roller coaster: filled with real and imagined danger, crammed with unexpected twists and turns, and resulting in stress, anxiety, and pain. When faced with danger, all breathing beings first gasp, hold their breath, and then breathe very shallowly. Only when perceived danger has passed do they exhale completely and begin returning to normal breathing patterns.

Even though it is instinctive behavior, holding our breath or breathing shallowly does not help us function optimally. Breath is the life force. Deprived of it, our brains slow down and our bodies and emotions panic and shout, "Red alert!" Holding your breath is a bodily response similar to emotionally tightly grasping something you fear losing. Being aware of your breathing, remembering to exhale, and resuming normal breathing as soon as possible is an effective way to accept the reality of right now.

Exhaling brings us the relief of relaxing, letting go, and releasing pent-up tension. Tears often have the same cleansing effect, as a Jewish proverb assures us: "What soap is for the body, tears are for the soul." Actually, tears also cleanse the body. Science has proven that tears shed as a result of difficult feelings such as grief and anger contain toxins, while tears flowing from positive feelings do not. How deeply and rhythmically you breathe is a conscious, mindful choice, as is allowing yourself the release of tears.

PRACTICE...

- Sit quietly with your eyes closed and gently focus on breathing in through your nose and out through your mouth for two or three minutes.

- Even if it is hard, give yourself permission to release any tears waiting to be shed. (In order to encourage tears to start, I may repeat "No!" several times and even pound on my bed.)

- In crisis, remember to breathe in and out.

THROUGHOUT YOUR DAY...

- Consciously even out your breath. Inhale to the count of five...Exhale to the count of five...

Both exhaling and crying make way for
the clean, fresh, and new.

TAKING AIM

If we could all follow Alfred P. Doolittle's advice in My Fair Lady when he sings, "When you chew on life's gristle, don't grumble, just whistle..." we'd be in fat city, so to speak. But often the worries and stresses of life's gristle get us down and seduce us into thinking we can—and should— somehow make everything better by finding ways to control the situation. Unfortunately, continuously chewing on a challenge usually doesn't solve it but simply makes it bigger and bigger and harder and harder to digest— reminds me of the ominous ickiness of chewing liver.

When we let worries consume us, they own us. They become the matrix around which our lives revolve. Since I know so well how easy it is to get lost in a maze of resistant worry, I asked a college friend how she escapes from the worry trap. The acronym for her steps is 'AIM;' her system helps me loosen worry's grip.

Awareness

Become aware of what you are gnawing on and how you feel about it. For instance, I can lose sleep worrying about my adult kids.

Insight

Without judgment, gain insight by observing how your worries and concerns are trapping you in an endless cycle of what-ifs, I-shoulds, and possibly some ain't-it-awfuls. Worry about my kids takes me out of the here and now and into places where I have no control—nor should I.

Make It Okay

Depending on what your heart resonates with, there are innumerable ways to make a gristly situation a smidgen more palatable. A powerful one is simply letting it be okay—allowing what is, not in a spirit of resignation or giving up, but with compassionate nonattachment, releasing resistance. To help me relax and let things be okay, I often use lovingkindness blessings, prayer, visualization, and ritual.

Recently, I threw leaves symbolizing my concerns into the stream behind our house. Fear, lack of trust, and sadness all rode the current downstream. As the leaves disappeared, I gave thanks for the idea of accepting what is and for what I know is true of my children: that they are strong, good, wise, and kind. Ritual and words both helped me regain my equilibrium.

PRACTICE...

- Take AIM—be aware, gain insight, make it okay through acceptance—whenever you get stranded in a maze of worry, anxiety, or fear.

THROUGHOUT YOUR DAY...

- Lovingly remind yourself that "this too shall pass."

Love yourself as you move toward
acceptance and beyond worry.

GIVING GRACE YOUR HAND

Grace is godlike goodness and respect given freely and unconditionally. Grace is a sense of divine love and protection bestowed on us when we need strength and renewal. Grace helps you know you are not alone and believe you are cared for and cherished. Grace is a drink of clear, clean water in the desert.

The grace of God, the grace of friendship, the grace of pets, the grace of competent and compassionate professionals, the grace of nature, the grace of hope, and the grace of angels surround us in all situations and circumstances. We, however, need to believe in the potential for grace and reach out our hearts to accept it from all who offer its solace and support.

I love the following assurance by author and theologian Frederick Buechner.

> The grace of God means something like: 'Here is your life. You might never have been, but you are because the party wouldn't have been complete without you. Here is the world. Beautiful and terrible things will happen. Don't be afraid. I am with you.

Nothing can ever separate us. It's for you I created the universe.
I love you.'

There's only one catch. Like any other gift, the gift of grace can
be yours only if you'll reach out and take it. Maybe being able
to reach out and take it is a gift too.

Whether or not you can reach out and take the gift of grace is determined
by your state of mind. Believing that grace is inaccessible or feeling you're
not worthy of receiving it blocks the flow of grace, which naturally longs to
come your way.

Feelings elicited by the gift of grace manifest differently for each of us.
Grace can feel as if you're enfolded in a loving hug. Or it may mean that
hope and a belief in possibilities break through a mind shrouded in
depression. Grace may unstick what was stuck in or around you. And
best of all, grace may give you the gift of really knowing you are loved
and lovable.

PRACTICE...

- Become aware of your feelings about the availability of grace.

- If you doubt the gift of grace, ask who within you doubts. Ask internal
  doubters what they want and need from you. If appropriate and
  loving, grant their wishes.

- Enhance belief by breathing in slowly while saying, "Thank you," and
  continue as you breathe out, "for the gift of grace."

- In times of need, reach out to grace by breathing in while saying, "I
  accept and welcome" and then breathe out, "the gift of grace."

THROUGHOUT YOUR DAY...

- Make a point to notice grace everywhere.

Swaying with the wind

A willow exemplifies

Grace-filled acceptance.

Overflowing from an Open Heart

An open heart bridges heaven and earth.

Being able to open your heart to yourself and others
and reopen it when it snaps shut in the face of danger, despair, and
disillusionment may be the greatest challenge of your lifetime. Because we
are vulnerable humans prone to defensiveness, opening our hearts is an
ongoing endeavor. With a genuine desire to keep your heart open as well as
a deep and accepting understanding of how difficult it can be, you can be
openhearted more often than not.

In the midst of a tough winter, my mood was as bleak as the post-blizzard
streets were ugly and hazardous. Things had not been going my way, and
I felt like a teeth-clenching, overstimulated, closed-hearted bitch whose
every nerve was exposed and jangling. Driving to an appointment in town,
I begged, "Please, angels, God, all my guides and guardians, I need help to
open my heart again!" Nothing happened: only my continual reassurance to
myself that awareness is the first step toward change.

While maneuvering the ice clogged streets, I saw a police car blocking a
right turn lane. As I approached, the reason for the car's position became
apparent. A policewoman was gently and cautiously helping an elderly
woman navigate the treacherously slippery crosswalk. This kindness
vignette was answered prayer and the beginning of my heart's much-
needed flow.

Our hearts naturally cycle between open and closed, frozen and flowing. It's
helpful to maintain a gentle climate of understanding during both.

STARTING A KINDNESS REVOLUTION

I like to think it's no accident that our species is called humankind.
Humankind! What if we—just you and me—made a commitment to
mindfully integrate kindness into each and every day of our lives? We

would start a kindness revolution. Let's do it. Let's become the proverbial pebbles in the pond and send ripples of kindness out into the world each day. Those whose hearts are touched by our kindness will hopefully be encouraged to pass it on, and then a revolution of much-needed kindness will have begun. Let's live up to our name by evolving into what it implies— humans who are consistently kind.

In his wonderfully friendly and openhearted way, the Dalai Lama is already a kindness revolutionary. He states, "This is my simple religion. There is no need for temples, no need for complicated philosophy. Our own brain, our own heart is our temple; the philosophy is kindness." One of the blessings of believing in a philosophy of kindness is that kindness opens the hearts of both giver and receiver.

Another great philosopher, Winnie the Pooh, is also among the ranks of those bringing kindness. He explains to a friend in the Thousand Acre Wood, "Just because an animal is large, it doesn't mean he doesn't want kindness; however big Tigger seems to be, remember that he wants as much kindness as Roo." Pooh's lesson is a good one to remember. No matter how big and tough someone looks, they want and need kindness as much as we do. As we start our powerfully heart-opening and heart-warming revolution of kindness, what better companions can we have than the Dalai Lama and Winnie the Pooh?

PRACTICE...

- Think big. We can have a huge influence.

- Act small. Each act of kindness, no matter how small, makes a big difference.

- Help yourself make a habit of integrating kindness into each day by posting a reminder like "Be Kind" where it is easily seen.

- Pause before acting or speaking and ask yourself, "What is kind in this situation?"

- Choose kindness.

- Give yourself a pat on the back in celebration of your own kindness and goodness. (Doing so boosts your belief in yourself and makes it easier to create a habit of kindness.)

THROUGHOUT YOUR DAY...

- Commit conscious acts of kindness.

Being kind in thought, word,
and deed opens your heart.

FINDING FREEDOM IN FORGIVENESS

Nothing slams your heart shut more resoundingly than holding a grudge, nursing a grievance, stewing in resentment, or resisting what was or what is. Not being able to forgive binds us to the original wound and to the one who wounded us. Remaining in a state of anger or hurt and—no matter how secretly—desiring revenge is akin to lugging around an internal cauldron of boiling bile hoping it will somehow scald the other person. It won't. But building up the bile of unforgiveness sure does hurt you. Holding onto an injustice blocks the flow of life's good energy, depletes your immune system, and makes it very difficult to experience laughter, love, and joy. Ironically, while lack of forgiveness greatly impacts us, it has little or no effect on the person with whom we are upset.

The idea that forgiveness is the best revenge could well be true. Forgiveness frees us from the past, empowers us to move on, and allows us to regain the ability to make fun, loving, and light-filled choices. Because of the enormous benefits to the one who forgives, forgiveness could almost be seen as a selfish act. It's definitely a self-loving act.

Which brings me to a fundamental aspect of forgiveness: the necessity to forgive yourself. Forgiving ourselves includes making amends to whomever we have offended or hurt, learning from our mistakes, and mindfully avoiding the same mistakes again. Forgiving yourself entails accepting the person you were at the time by realizing you would have acted or spoken differently if you had known how. Most of us need to forgive ourselves for things done or said unwittingly or thoughtlessly. On the other hand, if you consciously wound others, it can indicate deep-seated anger and injuries which may be beyond your ability to heal on your own. If this is true for you, please give yourself the gift of therapy.

PRACTICE...

- Without judgment, become aware of anyone you need to forgive, including yourself.

- As you breathe deeply and rhythmically, allow an image of the person to come into your mind's eye. Ask for divine love to flow into and through you toward them and silently say, "I forgive you and release my feelings of_____." (Visualizing the person as an innocent toddler often helps forgiveness flow. This technique can be especially valuable when forgiving parents.)

- Make amends if needed.

THROUGHOUT YOUR DAY...

- Affirm your commitment to forgive.

- Create personal rituals of release and forgiveness that bring you peace.

Forgiveness is freedom.

———————————

BEING A FRIEND

Having trusted friends is a must. Undoubtedly, many of our closest and dearest friends will be women because we usually want and need the same kind of heart connection and honest sharing of feelings.

True friends see who we really are, hear not only our words but the feelings behind them, hold us in the safe harbor of their embrace, and accept us as we are. Good friends mirror our best back to us, forgive our worst, and believe we will grow and evolve into wise, wacky, and wonderful old broads. Dear friends give us their undivided attention, support us during hard times, encourage us to laugh, and entice us into silliness. And we do the same for them.

A true friend gives us the courage to be ourselves because we know she is with us always and in all ways. In the safety of such friendships, our hearts can fully open.

I'm not sure how I would have survived the collapse of my first marriage without my women friends. One ranted and raved with me on the night I found out about my husband's betrayal, and together, we pretend-planned how to maim him in the most painful ways possible. We howled with laughter and with hurt, indignation, and downright terror on my part. And then she tucked me into bed. Throughout the long process of disentanglement, my friends encouraged me, comforted me, and finally kicked me in the buns and lovingly—with some well-founded impatience—told me to get on with it. They were right, and I followed their advice.

Ah, now the harder questions: Are you a trustworthy and devoted friend to yourself? Do you treat yourself with as much love and support as you do your three dearest friends? I would not have been able to answer yes to those questions before my divorce. My self-esteem was in the toilet and my fear levels off the charts. By continuing to befriend me when I felt like such a pitiful loser, women—and a wonderful man or two—helped me begin to believe in myself in a way I never had before. Learning to be my own dear friend was possibly the biggest blessing I gained from that painful experience.

PRACTICE...

- Consciously choose to treat yourself as well as you do your dear friends, even if it feels unnatural.

- Tell a friend how much you appreciate them.

THROUGHOUT YOUR DAY...

- Nurture friendships with kindness, understanding, empathy, and laughter.

- Connect with a friend in a small or large way.

Befriend yourself, and you naturally befriend others.

KNOWING YOU ARE LOVABLE AND LOVED

Trusting you are lovable and loved is one of the best ways to become openhearted. Feeling lovable and loved on the inside makes it easier to express love outwardly. If feeling loved and believing you are lovable is difficult for you, you can begin moving toward more positive beliefs and emotions by accepting, loving, and healing the child you once were. She lives within you and may still fear she is not worthy of love.

Until the age of six or seven, children think the entire world revolves around them; consequently, they tend to feel that they are the cause of anything that happens in their sphere. If a child received only unconditional love and could always rely on adults and the world not to disappoint her, that would be great, but such childhoods are rare. In the real world, things go awry and people are imperfect. By believing they cause all the bad stuff, children can come to the conclusion that they must be flawed and unlovable.

While you now know intellectually you were not to blame for the circumstances of your childhood, your inner little girl may carry residual shame from believing she was somehow bad. For instance, Shanti, a beautiful, wise, talented, and adventurous young woman I know, can lose sight of the woman she has become when the child within her is triggered by fear, failure, or insecurity. As the youngest child of a narcissistic, attacking mother, Shanti became her mother's favorite target and was repeatedly told she was a bad girl. Because she could not do anything well enough and could never count on her unpredictable mother, Shanti felt unsafe and insecure throughout her formative years.

Because of the depths of her wounds, it isn't easy for Shanti to feel lovable; however, I believe it will be natural for her one day because she is absolutely dedicated to healing her inner child and living as a strong, loving woman today.

A wounded heart is vulnerable yet capable of great compassion. All of us are wounded to some degree, and each of us has the ability to heal and open her heart. An open heart is a powerful emissary for all that is loving and good. Each open heart increases beauty and compassion in the cosmos.

PRACTICE...

- Quiet your mind by focusing solely on your breath for a few minutes.

- Visualize your inner little girl as happy, playful, and receiving all she wants and deserves.

- Bless any negative thoughts or images that arise. Bless them and let them be. Gently return to the here and now of your breath.

- Once again, see your inner child as happy and self-assured.

THROUGHOUT YOUR DAY...

- Love your inner child.

You are God's beloved daughter,
completely lovable and constantly loved.

GIVING GRATITUDE A GO

Gratitude is the golden key to opening your heart. Being grateful is paying attention to and appreciating life's treasures. Reveling in the blessings and riches life offers creates feelings of well-being, love, abundance, and delight. Highlighting and celebrating the positive encourages your heart to unfurl, much like warm sunlight prompts a flower to open.

As a sage once said, "Gratefulness creates great fullness." From great fullness, we can easily and effortlessly overflow onto Mother Earth and all her children. Giving from overflow is a gift without strings or expectations attached, whereas giving out of obligation when we feel drained can deplete us even more and be laced with exhaustion, resentment, or anger.

Paradoxically, when we feel empty and purposeless, selfless giving is often exactly what we need to do in order for our hearts to experience great fullness. Giving to others who are less fortunate or are going through a hard time activates gratitude within us—gratitude for our own blessings and for being able to be of service. We also gain inspiration from people who courageously survive adversity. If you are feeling drained or empty, quiet your mind and gently pay attention to your needs. In thoughtful quietness, clarity can come, and you will know whether reaching out or going within is needed to provide balance right now.

As a mindfulness practice, or to fill yourself up when running on empty, try giving gratitude a go. Having an attitude of gratitude reminds us of our source and reconnects us to the essence of Spirit. As a French proverb explains, "Gratitude is the heart's memory." Awakening to gratitude and remembering all you have to be thankful for, places you in the embrace of the Divine, where your heart can open and overflow as naturally as a spring flows from its source.

PRACTICE...

- Set the intention to give gratitude a go each day.

- Before getting out of bed in the morning, be grateful for another day of life. Follow with a simple prayer, such as:

- Thank you for all experiences and feelings waiting for me today. Please help me keep my heart open and grant me the wisdom to handle everything with grace, humor, happiness, and strength.

- During the day, consciously replace fear-based thoughts with ones of gratitude and joy.

- Before drifting off to sleep at the end of the day, think of at least two people, experiences, or things for which you are grateful. Reexperience the sweet feelings as deeply as you can.

THROUGHOUT YOUR DAY...

- Each hour, take a moment to fully notice something for which you are grateful.

Gratitude fills a thirsty heart to overflowing.

EXPECTING GOOD

Intangible thoughts, expectations, and beliefs are powerful, magnetic realities drawing to us energy and experiences that match what we send out. Expecting good is issuing an invitation to the universe to send more good your way. For instance, if you expect your day to be a good one, chances are it will be. If you expect it to be lousy, the amendable universe often makes sure your expectation is met.

There are times when believing good is already here or expecting it is on the way doesn't seem to make any noticeable difference in your life. Patience is needed because our time and God's time often differ. Also, the Divine's way of providing our good can certainly look different than we expect it to look. In fact, it sometimes appears as if God loves a scavenger hunt and delights in hiding my good deep in what at first appears to be manure.

If I had known a psychotherapy practice and a writing career would evolve from the struggles life generously provided, would I have resisted the pain less? I don't know, but from the wisdom of hindsight, I do know that adversity made me a stronger woman and provided the impetus to create two careers I'm passionate about and I hope help the world a little.

It's much easier to expect good when you believe God (or whatever you call the Divine) is benevolent and wants only good for you. I've grown to agree with author Max Lucado's opinion about how much God loves us. He says, "If God had a refrigerator, your picture would be on it." The optimist I've intentionally become attempts to expect a good outcome, an important lesson, or an opportunity for inspiration to come from all occurrences. When I can't do that, I pay attention to my breath and stay safely anchored in the present moment as much as possible.

PRACTICE...

- Quietly become aware of your breath.

- Easily and gently deepen your breath.

- Return to normal breathing and imagine breathing in and out from your heart center.

- On the in-breath affirm, "God loves me," on the out-breath affirm, "And so do I."

- With your hands palm up on your lap, request, "Please help me to cradle, not clutch, each person, feeling, and experience that comes my way today."

THROUGHOUT YOUR DAY...

- Be aware of and appreciate even the smallest good that comes to you.

Expect, notice, and accept good.

BEING A CHEERLEADER

Recently, while pondering my purpose in life, a surprising thought popped into my head. "You're a cheerleader." No, wait, that answer is about fifty years and a whole lot of flexibility too late…But the more I thought about being a cheerleader, the better I liked the idea. Don't you love to be cheered on in your endeavors? Isn't it great to receive a rousing "Attagirl!" when you score a success? And doesn't it help relieve the feeling of being all alone when a supportive friend comes to your defense when you're being mistreated?

Aware of my own yearning to be cheered on as a girl and as a young woman, somewhere along the line I made a conscious decision to cheer others on. At first, I had to remind myself to applaud and approve of others, and yes, to consistently and nonjudgmentally give myself the accolades I'd felt deprived of growing up and in my first marriage.

Luckily, several of the women I was close to at the time also needed cheerleaders. We supported each other to the point of sometimes yelling, "Standing ovation! Standing ovation!" which meant the woman who wanted and needed cheering was to stand and bow in response to our shouts of approval. Giving and receiving standing ovations was rowdy fun and surprisingly rewarding for both applauder and applaudee—probably because our hearts open more fully when we help others feel good about themselves.

Accentuating the positive by seeing and appreciating the good in others, within yourself, and in the world draws additional goodness to you. In his newsletter, meditation teacher and author James Baraz agrees that cheerleading can call forth goodness: "We have great power to draw out the goodness from others if we look for it. Try looking for what is good in others and in life around you. The way to do this is by having your radar out for what you appreciate about them. Most people will sense this very easily and will relax around you as well as let their goodness more naturally shine."

PRACTICE...

- Pay attention to your desire for approval and provide it to yourself unstintingly. It's perfectly okay to give yourself a standing ovation.

- Look for the good in others and shower them with appreciation, encouragement, and applause.

- "Listen and attend with the ear of your heart," as Saint Benedict urges.

THROUGHOUT YOUR DAY...

- Find reasons to celebrate yourself and others.

Illuminated by the light of appreciation and approval, we shine.

ACTING LOVINGLY

Love takes many forms; romantic, physical, altruistic, parental, familial, and impersonal, to name just a few. All are good in the right time and setting. Love emanates from the center of your heart, and scientists now know that the heart is the most powerful organ in your body, both physically and energetically. As the highest form of heart energy, love is amazingly powerful. When we learn to choose what feels right in our hearts rather than what is logical to the mind, we will change the world in magical, transformative, and healing ways.

Two women I know have started transforming their worlds already. Anne's motto is, "Love: Be it. Say it. Do it." As a survivor of cancer, she has honed what is important down to one thing: Love. To the best of her ability, she says it, does it, and is learning to be it more each day. Colleen concentrates on opening her heart and spreading love by asking, "What would Love do?" when faced with almost any question or action. I might add, "What is the kind response, action, or attitude for this time and setting?"

In Part I, I spoke about the insight progression our practices were designed to facilitate. It looks like this:

Insight → Awareness → Action

While it's wonderful to be mindful about asking what Love would do, it's only the first step. Asking gives you insight about what would be loving, awareness lets you know how you feel about the insight gained. Can you happily follow your heart's advice, or do you feel resistant about heeding Love's counsel? It really doesn't matter which it is; the crucial step is the next one: choosing to act in a loving manner no matter how you feel.

Interestingly, the energy of love is so powerful that it often boomerangs back to us, creating warm, cozy feelings even when we act from choice rather than feeling. Choosing an act of love can open your heart to the feelings of love.

PRACTICE...

- Set an intention to act lovingly.

- Before reacting to a situation or person, take a few mindful breaths. Ask, "What would love do?" Listen to your heart.

- If you are still in doubt about a response at that point, give yourself the gift of time and acceptance. Breathe gently into your heart whenever thoughts of the dilemma come to mind and relax into the awareness that in the fullness of time, you will know how love wants to act through you.

THROUGHOUT YOUR DAY...

- Choose to be, say, and do love.

Opening your heart,
A gift of mindfulness that
Spreads lovingkindness.

Generating Soft Power

At the center of your being you have the answer; you know who you are, and you know what you want.

———————————————

—Lao-tzu

As bearers and givers of life, women are incredibly strong and amazingly powerful; we hold the center around which our families revolve. Some of you have probably recognized and claimed your innate strength and influence more gracefully than I did. When I began gaining a sense of empowerment, I also noticed myself growing a tougher-than-necessary shell. It was as if I felt the need for a steel exoskeleton to house my newfound power and hold me upright in the face of opposition from those who preferred I remain acquiescent and malleable. I wasn't alone in my crustiness. Many of my newly assertive clients and friends were also experiencing unfamiliar and uncomfortable tight-jawed toughness.

The adage "When the student is ready, the teacher will appear" came true for me at a friend's croning ceremony; several women gathered to honor a friend who had attained the age and gathered the wisdom of an elder, or "crone." When the facilitator mentioned the term "soft power" during the ritual, a light went on within me. In that moment, I realized I had sacrificed the soft-edged, openhearted, ready-to-embrace aspects of myself on the altar of empowerment. During that flash of insight, I also understood I could have both.

Softness and empowerment complement each other. However, soft power can be distorted by unfinished business, limiting beliefs, old wounds, and fear. By mindfully and lovingly clearing away emotional debris and honoring our authentic selves, we can bless those we care about—and the world in general—by naturally generating and expressing the soft power that is our fundamental nature.

TYING UP LOOSE ENDS

Unfinished business swirls in our minds like psychic flotsam and jetsam, making a quiet, powerful mind almost impossible to attain. All the niggling beliefs about what you should have done, regrets about what you did or didn't do, or lingering feelings about what was done to you drain energy from the here and now by flinging your attention into the future or sinking it back into the past. Since all life truly resides in the moment, floating fragments of old, unfinished business exhaust rather than empower you.

One of the most effective ways of tying up loose ends is to do what can be done to bring closure. If taxes are due, complete them. If you need to make amends, do so to the best of your ability. If emotional baggage is weighing you down or trapping you in the past, find a therapist or friend who can help you heal, release, and let be. Throughout the process of finishing business and freeing yourself from draining thoughts, support yourself with acceptance and appropriate action.

Because our minds tend to get in a groove and replay the "oldies and baddies"—like real or imagined failures, wounds, guilts, and resentments— we need to find ways to change the station and claim our innate soft power. Continually thinking about what makes us feel bad is an indication we have become overly attached to our personal stories and possibly even addicted to the adrenaline produced by rehashing them. Old stories and the accompanying feelings can become your false identity. However, changing obsessive thoughts, tying up loose ends, and letting go of the past can help you become the softly empowered woman you can be now.

The breath practice below is designed to help free your mind from the grasp of unfinished business. Noticing thoughts neutrally and immediately releasing them breaks the bonds of habitual thinking and helps you recognize your authentic self in the present moment.

PRACTICE...

- With your eyes closed, focus solely on your breath. Breathe naturally.

- When thoughts come, acknowledge them with a neutral word such as "thinking." Immediately return your attention to your breath. (It's not unusual to repeat this process many times during a ten-minute session.)

- Do not judge your practice as good or bad. Simply acknowledge yourself for doing it.

- The keys to success are practice and neutrality.

THROUGHOUT YOUR DAY...

- Do small things to tie up loose ends.

Your point of power is in the present moment.

ACCESSING BODY WISDOM

Wouldn't it be wonderful to have a wise and intuitive counselor available twenty-four seven? You're in luck; you already have one: your body! Our bodies carry an ancient wisdom. We literally live within a temple of intuitive and instinctual wisdom. Sometimes we pay attention and access body wisdom; but unfortunately, the aphorism "Mrs. Smith lived a short distance from her body" is sadly true for many of us.

Bernie Siegel, noted author and physician, believes our bodies are far more complex and fascinating than we give them credit for and that many patients who successfully access body wisdom triumph over illness and fear. Of the people who heal miraculously, Dr. Siegel says, "They focus on the meaning of their life and their divine essence, and they live it. They do not project their problems onto others but seek to make a beautiful world and create goodness in their relationships." The body and mind are inextricably linked; what affects one affects the other. Dr. Siegel puts it this way, "Our problem lies in our ability to think and worry." Negative thinking and worry stifle your body's natural inclination toward health and wisdom. In its ideal state, the body can be likened to clear, clean spring water flowing sweetly from the breast of Mother Earth. Even when contaminated with tainted substances, spring water will cleanse itself. Of course, a spring needs time free from contaminants in order to stay clean, just as our physical, emotional, mental, and spiritual bodies need time free from dirty, disabling thoughts of fear and resentment in order to operate optimally.

Not only is your body a temple filled with wisdom, but it is also the one vehicle that carries you through life. The physical vehicle needs upkeep, care, good food, exercise, water, medical attention, and time to rest and rejuvenate. The wisdom temple needs positive thoughts and attitudes to keep it clean and sparkly. And, the body temple thrives best when attention is paid to its innate wisdom. Accessing the body's wisdom can be as simple as acknowledging the need for a nap and taking one, if possible, or it can be as miraculous as transforming a life-threatening illness into a life well lived.

PRACTICE...

- Direct your attention and breath to your body. Breathe deeply into areas that are experiencing pain, tightness, or discomfort of any kind.

- As you breathe into challenging areas, thank them for all they do for you. Imagine breathing relaxation and healing into those spaces.

- Rest a moment in the wisdom of your body temple.

THROUGHOUT YOUR DAY...

- Notice and listen to your body.

Body wisdom: Notice early; honor immediately.

REELING IN PROJECTIONS

An excellent indicator of soft power is having the maturity to take responsibility for your own feelings and behavior. Denying what lives inside us does not make it go away. Unidentified and unresolved feelings slip into hiding, like snakes going under a rock, where they wait until provoked to strike out, generally with inappropriate and wounding behavior. Unfortunately, those struck are often our loved ones.

Walloping someone else over the head with your own issues is called projection. The act of projecting can be described by using the analogy of a movie projector. Unaware of the subject matter of a film or video, a projector automatically shines the contents onto a blank screen. The person with hidden issues is the projector, her buried feelings are the content of the film or video, and the person projected upon is the blank screen hit by others' pent-up energy.

As an example, my client lovingly and responsibly cared for her father for months before his death. Her dad's generation believed real men were strong, silent, and always in charge. Because he was intelligent, handsome, and accomplished, he never felt the need to be aware of or heal his more vulnerable feelings. Emotional wounds sustained in war were buried along with all others, including the fear of decline and death. As Marg's father became weaker and more dependent, the energy of unresolved issues began to erupt. Feelings hidden for many years were now projected onto Marg as her failures. Even though she understood the psychological underpinnings of the attacks, Marg was understandably devastated by them.

Because most of us are not yet fully enlightened, we will occasionally project onto others. However, we can reel in the vast majority of our projections by discovering, healing, and taking responsibility for hidden feelings. If you do wound someone by word or action, diligently search for and examine feelings of your own that might have provoked the behavior. Bring troublesome feelings into the light of awareness and work on transforming them with love. Mend relationships by acknowledging unfair projections and sincerely apologizing.

PRACTICE...

- Before saying anything that could be hurtful, pause. Breath… Breathe…Breathe…

- Pause a while longer. Breathe into your heart.

- In a nonjudgmental way, ask, "Could this be about me?"

- If so, gently explore your feelings with the goal of understanding and transforming them.

- Project acceptance onto yourself and others.

Project the light of love into the world.

———————————————

NOTICING WHAT'S RIGHT

Roaming in the dark underworld of fear—which is easy to do if we immerse ourselves in news and social media—makes it almost impossible to notice what is right with the world and our own lives. While it's important to be aware of, attempt to understand, and take constructive action against injustice, inequality, and downright wrong happenings, it is also essential to see and absorb the good, kind, and beautiful around and in us—we need to take in what is right, right here, right now!

Sages, scientists, and psychologists agree all life needs balance: a balance of light and dark, heavy and heart-lifting, hope and uncertainty, altruism and self-care. Without balance, we—and our entire world—can become dangerously off kilter, out of sync, disassociated, and cruel. Our society is in the midst of an unbalanced time, which makes it crucial for us to notice what is right amid the myriad wrongs. Being aware of what is right helps us maintain personal balance and energetically assists others—including Mother Earth—in regaining balance. I know it sounds simplistic, but sound science is often simple.

In order for students to be happy and effective, His Holiness the Dalai Lama encourages them to "focus on what is healthy and productive rather than wrong, diseased, and destructive." You, too, can be healthier, happier, and more powerful when you balance acknowledging and working toward changing what is wrong with concentrating on and celebrating what is right within and around you.

PRACTICE...

- Before getting out of bed, close your eyes for a moment and remember something good about your night's sleep.

- During a meal, notice a particularly pleasing taste. Focus on enjoying it.

- A few times during your day, close your eyes and concentrate on your breath loyally moving in and out of your body. Feel or sense the beat of your heart. Give thanks for the rhythm and flow of life.

THROUGHOUT YOUR DAY...

- Note at least three good, kind, or beautiful things close at hand.

Noticing what is right is empowering and uplifting.

VALUING AUTHENTICITY OVER PERFECTION

Authenticity is possible, perfection is not.

As author Hugh Prather says, "Perfectionism is slow death." That sounds dramatic, but for those of us who hold ourselves, or know others who hold us, to a standard of perfection, his words ring true. One of the definitions of perfect is "conforming absolutely to the description of an ideal type without flaws, defects or shortcomings." By definition, no one I know is perfect, but many are interestingly and lovingly authentic.

Empowered, genuine people realize that everyone has a combination of strengths and vulnerabilities as well as virtues and vices and therefore accept their own. In reality, accepting your strengths and virtues—your genuine goodness—is sometimes harder than owning and expressing vulnerability and vice. But honoring and sharing your unique talents and qualities is an indispensable step toward generating the soft power of authenticity. Living authentically can make the world a more loving, honest, and respectful place. As teacher Dugpa Rinpoche encourages, "Do not doubt your own inner splendor. Each living being is a star."

How does your star shine? What gifts do you bring to family, friends, and your own corner of the battered and bruised world? With Covid-19 plus massive injustice and inequity fermenting all around us, a group of my friends came together via Zoom to ruminate about ways to help make things better. Inhibited by the realities of quarantine, we didn't come up with a concrete list of To Dos out in the world, but we did have a heartfelt and uplifting sharing about our authentic gifts and how they might be used for greater personal and global good. We ended the meeting more aware of our individual skills and enthused about doing what we can with what is available to us right here and now.

As our Zoom circle did, women can help each other act authentically and recognize their innate goodness. The good news is that seeing, being, and doing what reflects your heart's genuine gifts also invites helpfulness, empowerment, and kindness into your life.

PRACTICE...

- Take inventory of your gifts, strengths and admirable qualities.

- While sitting for practice, breathe in "I am" (or "I have") and breathe out one of your gifts, strengths, or qualities. (As an example, breathe in, "I have" and breathe out "a gift for listening.")

THROUGHOUT YOUR DAY...

- Notice whether your thoughts, words, and actions ring true with your heart.

Get real.

FINDING AND USING YOUR VOICE

Finding their own unique voice is a huge issue for many women. As a teenager and a twentysomething, I continually cleared my throat and felt as if I were choking much of the time. I was. I was choking back words I thought people wouldn't like to hear, choking on feelings I labeled bad, choking on self-judgment—choking on shoulds, have-tos, and fears. Not only were the reasons for clearing my throat limiting, but the physical act itself was annoying and played havoc with some of my more promising dates.

In order to keep my throat clear, I needed to find my voice. To this day, learning to speak out in softly empowered ways is a continuing process for me. One day, Anna, a client who had been working on finding her voice, came bounding into my office bubbling with excitement. Hardly able to contain herself, she said, "Yesterday when I was trying to express myself to my husband, he told me to crawl back in my hole." Pausing to laugh heartily, she proudly exclaimed, "I told him 'I can't. I filled it in!' " By daring to speak up, Anna was exhilarated and empowered.

While many women have found their authentic voices and do not feel the need to silence themselves, some of us may still need a little encouragement. Not only does your voice express beliefs, ideas, and creativity unique to you, it also carries its own unique vibration. Using your voice as an expression of authenticity sends a vibration of honesty and trustworthiness into the atmosphere, where laws of nature cause those qualities to expand. Voices are powerful tools. Used mindfully and lovingly, your voice can have a healing impact in both the microcosm of your intimate circles and the macrocosm of the world.

Understandably, our voices can ring out with goodness and wisdom only when we trust that wisdom and goodness live within us. Noted meditation teacher Pema Chodron uses her voice to invite us to be curious about ourselves in a light and loving way. "Meditation is a process of lightening up, of trusting the basic goodness of what we have and who we are, and realizing that any wisdom that exists, exists in what we already have. The key is to wake up, to become more alert, more inquisitive and curious about ourselves."

Just as a candle flame can be seen clearly in the darkness, one peaceful, loving voice can be heard amid even hate and horror. May our voices be among the peacemakers.

- Place half of your attention on your breath and half on noticing aspects of yourself active now. Whether dark or light, healthy or wounded, nonjudgmentally notice the aspects as they surface.

- Gently acknowledge who needs to speak out and who needs to be quieter.

- Give yourself permission to find your voice and choose to use it with empowered honesty.

THROUGHOUT YOUR DAY...

- Speak your truth kindly and lovingly.

- Or choose to stay silent from integrity, not fear.

Mindful choice gives rise to thoughtful, genuine expression.

ERRING ON THE SIDE OF GENEROSITY

Being generous is beneficial to both giver and receiver. In fact, the benefits gained from being generous are so great, it's fair to say generosity is self-loving as well as altruistic. A recipient of someone else's generosity gets items and attitudes valuable to them whereas the giver is blessed by the positive feelings associated with openheartedness.

One form of generosity about which we've already spoken is kindness, but because I think it's impossible to tout kindness too often, I want to share two quotes I love that align generosity with kindness. The first is from author Robert Brault: "Today I bent the truth to be kind, and I have no regret, for I am far surer of what is kind than I am of what is true." Since I, too, am far surer of kindness than truth, this quote resonated with my heart. The next wisdom is from Ralph Waldo Emerson: "You can never do a kindness too soon, for you never know how soon it will be too late." Right! If you've ever delayed an act of kindness or generosity until it was too late, as I have, you know the sadness that clenches your heart as a result.

Believing the best about people, and therefore, giving them the benefit of the doubt, is another form of generosity that opens your heart. Believing in someone before all the facts are in is akin to being innocent until proven guilty. If you've experienced being misjudged, you can truly appreciate the value of judging others favorably. The other day, a woman I know accused me of something I would never even consider doing. "Don't you know me better than that?" I wanted to ask but didn't feel safe enough to do so. Although she later apologized, the experience remains a visceral lesson about how painful it is to be judged harshly and unfairly.

I am actually really thankful to have experienced such an invaluable reminder to give others the benefit of the doubt. As you've probably already guessed, I have a hefty judge persona who can use all the lessons in slow judgment and fast forgiveness she can get.

To facilitate opening your heart—the seat of soft power—give yourself and others the gift of erring on the side of generosity.

PRACTICE...

- Calm and center your body and mind by concentrating on your breath for a few minutes.

- If there is anyone you are judging or anyone you feel judged by, allow an awareness of them to float into your consciousness.

- Inhale divine love and acceptance into your heart center; exhale the same divine love toward the person you are visualizing. The person can also be you.

- Be aware of and thankful for kindness and generosity extended to you.

Choose kindness and generosity.

TRANSFORMING FEAR

The single most empowering thing we can do for ourselves is to transform fear.

While fear contains tremendous power, it doesn't propel us forward and upward; but instead, it drags us down and chains us to the past. Freeing ourselves from the grasp of fear is a loving intention, because as fear subsides, we are better able to access the soft, sweet power of our hearts, which naturally leads to loving ourselves and others more freely and completely.

We are naturally curious, not naturally fearful. A baby is born with only two natural fears: fear of falling and fear of loud noises. All other fears, including the fear of death, are learned. Thankfully, what has been learned can be unlearned.

We are not our fear—we simply experience it. Please, never accept a definition of yourself that identifies you as your fear. Fear is not something we are but something we have. For example, you may have told yourself, "I'm such a loser." Although you may feel fearful and unsuccessful at times, it doesn't mean you're a loser—just the opposite. Any mindful attempt made to transform fear makes you a wise and courageous winner.

The following practice is called disidentification. It's exactly what the name implies: a technique to help us take a step back and realize that fear (and other emotions and thoughts) is not who we are but something we have and can change. Disidentification often dilutes the power of fear.

PRACTICE...

- Think of some sentences that appeal to you as definitions of who you are now or who you want to become. For example:

   ☒   I am a loving and lovable woman.

   ☒   I am a wise and compassionate friend.

   ☒   I am perfectly okay just as I am at this moment.

- When fear arises, pay attention to it, name it, and then repeat several times, "I have a fear of (fill in the blank here: failure, heights, abandonment, blind dates), but I am not this fear."

- Take a moment to consciously breathe in the fact that you are much more than any fear you have. Exhale any vestiges of the named fear into the atmosphere and imagine it being transformed into light and love.

THROUGHOUT YOUR DAY...

- Transform fearful energy into positive by affirming what you are. Add a sentence of your choosing to the disidentification statement. For instance, I might say, "I have a fear of rejection, but I am not this fear. I am a unique and loving daughter of the Divine."

- I have a fear of _____, but I am not this fear. I am _____.

Courageous women

Transform fearfulness into

Loving energy.

_____

Inviting Serenity Through Simplicity

It does not matter whether one paints a picture, writes a poem, or carves a statue, simplicity is the mark of a master hand.

—Elise De Wolfe

Simplicity is a natural by-product of mindfulness. By concentrating attention on one person, feeling, activity, or thing, we invite extraneous and intrusive mind chatter to fade into the background. What remains is awareness of the moment: the pure and simple experience of life as it evolves moment by precious moment.

Just as mindfulness simplifies our internal environment, it is also useful in simplifying our physical surroundings. Being mindful of items we treasure and use regularly, and noticing those that have become superfluous, can guide our choices about what to keep and what to recycle.

We often feel more peaceful and balanced as a result of simplifying our lives.

Simplicity is calming. Simplicity is satisfying.

Simplifying creates inner and outer space, and space invites serenity.

OVERLOADING EVOLUTION

Drs. Rick Hanson and Rick Mendius—whose research on the brain's tendency to emphasize negative experiences over positive ones was mentioned in Part I—believe that our brains have not evolved sufficiently to absorb and process the rapid-fire stimuli they are constantly bombarded with in our warp-speed, tech-loving society. Since none of us are androids like Star Trek: The Next Generation's Commander Data, is it any wonder we often feel like overstimulated two-year-olds in desperate need of a nap?

Hopefully, the following computer-overload analogy shared by my son Brett will help assuage any guilt you may have over simplifying.

> As Mom was discussing the concept of information overload and the fact our brains have not yet evolved to a point that allows them to handle the vast amount of stimuli constantly assaulting our senses, it occurred to me that computers have experienced a similar evolutionary challenge. The neocortex of the brain and the RAM (random-access memory) of a computer act as the organizational processing centers of the brain and computer, respectively. The amount of RAM on a computer determines how fast it can work and how many functions it can do at once.
>
> The first personal computers were equipped with relatively small amounts of RAM. At that time, with no internet and limited demands for information processing, those computers worked just fine. With the appearance of the internet, the borders of information availability were blasted beyond our wildest imagination and existing computers quickly became obsolete. Any attempt to process more than one or two applications at a time either slowed your computer to a crawl or locked it up completely.

As it was with the computer, so it is with our organic equivalent. The stimuli and information flooding us on a daily basis have reached such epic proportions that our brains simply can't keep up. The more we struggle to keep pace—because that's what the world expects of us—the more our brains begin to strain…slow down…and can even lock up. So be gentle with your brain. If you allow it to handle just one thing at a time with great focus and care, I think you will be relieved and amazed at how well it still performs.

PRACTICE...

- If you feel overloaded and overwhelmed, relax your body and mind by taking several deep breaths.

- Appreciate your brain for the wonders it performs each moment.

- With love and respect for yourself, let go of unrealistic expectations.

THROUGHOUT YOUR DAY...

- Adopt a simple and kind, bite-sized approach to learning and life.

Live gently with yourself and your brain.

MOVING AT YOUR OWN PACE

Because of external demands, you may have lost track of your natural pace, the tempo of living that resonates best with your being. I know my internal Energizer Bunny remained ignorant of my natural pace for decades, and I overdid, over-planned, and over-pleased long after it was no longer necessary. I had become so accustomed to the exhaustion, tight jaws, and hyper-alertness of my daily life that it grew to be the norm.

I was shocked a few years ago to discover that my natural pace was much slower than I thought. In fact, I thrive best when limiting outside activities to two per day. At my stage of life, that's doable; during the "kid" years—with or without a pandemic—it would have been more difficult. I found my true tempo due to an unexpected surgery that forced me to come to a complete halt and then move through the recovery period slowly. To my surprise, I loved the unhurried pace. For me, Lily Tomlin was right when she proposed, "For fast-acting relief, try slowing down."

Having been "hogtied and throw'd on the ground," as they say in parts of my home state, I discovered many blessings in feeling underwhelmed. Less stress, bitchiness, and resentment and more laughs, relaxation, and naps were a few of them. Undoubtedly, the major blessing was the awareness that I'm a medium-paced woman, not the fast-paced one I expected myself to be.

The other day a wonderful young woman who gives me professional therapeutic massages said, "I've got such a good story to tell you!" Donia shared that she'd been working too hard and was exhausted and even feeling resentful toward clients. A few days before we spoke, Donia was crying on the way to a client's house because she hadn't made the time to say goodbye to a friend who'd died that day. "And you know what, Sue?" she said with a knowing grin. "I was reaching for a tissue and ran my car into a brick wall!"

Donia immediately interpreted the accident as a clear message to stop, find her natural pace, and honor it. Being a mindful woman, Donia adopted an attitude of gratitude and promised herself to begin moving at her own pace.

Please be kind to yourself by discovering and honoring your natural rhythm and pace.

PRACTICE...

- Nonjudgmentally, pay attention to feeling overwhelmed. Does it come from doing too much? Trying to be too much for too many?

Overscheduling? Not allowing yourself to rest enough? An unmet need for solitude?

- Honor your inner knowing about the perfect, right pace for you.

- When possible, schedule only those activities that elicit a "Yes!" from your heart.

THROUGHOUT YOUR DAY...

- Take time for literal breathers. Pause between tasks, at stoplights, or while waiting for kids, and take several deep, slow breaths. Imagine energy coming into your body and tension flowing out.

Carve out much-needed times of underwhelm.

LUBRICATING LIFE WITH TIME

The late author Hugh Prather was one of the nicest, most laid-back men I've met. Yet his writings revealed that he, too, needed to be mindful in order not to lose his good nature by overcommitting and rushing. He wrote, "I notice that when I place myself under a time constraint, when I set a deadline and rush to meet it, it's virtually impossible to keep from outwardly blaming or mentally attacking other people. Yet time can be a lubricant as well as a point of friction. Today I will give myself, my mind, and all that I do more than enough time."

Being overly familiar with time—or the shortage of it—as a point of friction, I love the concept of time as a lubricant! The picture that popped into my mind while reading about him giving himself more than enough time was that of a small moat surrounding activities, a watery decompression chamber on which to float before moving on to the next thing.

Water is a wonderful symbol of relaxation and rejuvenation to me, but something else may be more calming for you. If you are a nature lover, either imagining a few moments in a forest clearing or actually going outside might help you catch your breath, depressurize, and prepare for the next thing you want or need to do. Or perhaps, simply deciding to give yourself more than enough time will make it happen.

Of course, there are women who love being as busy as possible. If you thrive on back-to-back activities or are energized by having a packed schedule, you are probably one of them. That's great, as long as you're keeping the pace you want to, not one that you (or others) feel you should maintain. Most of us, however, feel the friction of time pressure at least some of the time and can benefit from simplifying our lives in ways that give us time to truly enjoy all that we do.

We are not, after all, slaves to the schedules we create. With awareness, self-care, and planning, we can lubricate our lives with the stress-reducing pleasure of enough time.

PRACTICE...

- Take time to muse about how it would feel to have enough time. Mindfully explore such questions as these: Do I need fewer obligations? Would more time alone be good? How can I create space and time between activities? What can I do to simplify my life in ways that feel self-nurturing?

- At least once this week, simplify your life in a way that gives you more than enough time.

- If having enough time brings a modicum of serenity, give yourself the gift of making it a habit.

THROUGHOUT YOUR DAY...

· Lubricate your life with a few well-timed free minutes.

Surround tasks and activities with time.

OPTING FOR SIMPLICITY OF THOUGHT

Simplicity of thought enhances warmth of heart.

I believe our instinctual nature is to feel great warmth and love toward ourselves, others, and the natural world; to be open to all people and things we encounter. Babies and puppies are good examples of inborn openness. Unless they've learned to be fearful or cautious, babies will smile upon the best and the worst. The same concept is true for puppies. Some very effective puppy training schools are housed in prisons. Inmates do the preliminary socialization and obedience training for service dogs, and the dogs unconditionally love their trainers. Many of the inmates involved begin believing in their dogs and end up believing in themselves, perhaps for the first time.

Babies and dogs don't let tangled thoughts overshadow their natural inclination to love and trust. When not mistreated or traumatized, they remain free from mind-clutter and as a result, they are able to spread great warmth and love in their wake. With a bit of mindful decluttering, so can you.

How and what we think is one of the few things over which we have control. Prem Rawat, also known as Maharaji, a very appealing teacher on inner peace since the age of eight, says, "The gift of thinking is one of the greatest gifts that God has given you, but what you think about is your gift to yourself." I know it's possible to give yourself the gift of simple, positive thinking because I retrained myself to do it. My mother was a wonderful woman, but she was bedeviled by worry much of the time. And I was an apt apprentice.

I use the following techniques to simplify both my inner and outer lives. At first glance they may seem too simplistic to work, but they are powerful tools. The scope of The Woman's Book of Mindfulness requires brevity. If you'd like to pursue these methods in depth, please see my book The Courage to Be Yourself.

PRACTICE...

- Pick a simple, positive statement and repeat it to override turbulent thoughts and worries.

- Two of my sentences are: "I can do all things through God who strengthens me" and "I am a lovable and good woman even though I make mistakes."

- Adopt the popular KISS (Keep It Simple, Sweetie) philosophy by mindfully simplifying and sweetening your thoughts.

THROUGHOUT YOUR DAY...

- Simply love yourself.

Simple thoughts and deeds invite a
quiet mind and warm heart.

BEING FOR, NOT AGAINST

It takes a lot of energy to get riled up over anything—politics, the state of our country's schools, healthcare, our own health, real or imagined slights from friends or mates, and whatever maddens you personally. Not only do we expend an exorbitant amount of energy getting riled up, it also leads to overproduction of bile by the liver, which hinders rather than helps digestion and can lead to gallstones among other ailments. Being chronically worried and upset promotes emotional discomfort and physical disease.

A while ago, I was touched by a squib in USA Today. ESPN's Peter Gammons shared that following his recovery from a brain aneurysm, the same condition that had killed his sister eleven years earlier, he doesn't worry much anymore. He said, "You know what it's like on talk radio, how people get so upset? Well, now I'm focused on what I'm for, not what I'm against. That's sort of my new life motto, 'What I'm for.' " How wonderfully simple.

I noticed Mr. Gammon decided to focus on what he's for, not against. While he might not word it this way, he's become more mindful of where he puts his attention.

I don't think anyone would disagree that there is much in the world that bears changing, but what if we changed our attitude toward it? Instead of being against the way schools are run, let's be for children getting the best education and vote accordingly, volunteer in the classroom when possible, and see that teachers get the salaries they deserve. For those of us aghast at the thought of war and the pain it inflicts on so many, we can be for peace. And we can be for those whose lives have been torn apart by war and do what we can to ease their pain. For example, we can write to the wounded and to our congresspersons, donate to good causes, reach out to widows and their children, or visit hospitals.

Being for something creates an upswing of energy and love that being against does not. Being for empowers and lightens, being against depletes and darkens. Being for is simply openhearted and embracing.

PRACTICE...

- If you become aware of feeling or speaking against something, pause. If it's safe, softly close your eyes and take two deep breaths. Direct your next three breaths to your heart.

- Ask yourself, "What can I be for in this?"

THROUGHOUT YOUR DAY...

- Focus on what you're for.

Being for brightens your day and lightens your heart.

DISCOVERING
SIMPLE SOLUTIONS

While there are definitely problems and injustices not easily solved, there are also hundreds of simple solutions to many of life's annoyances; but often they seem to hover just outside our awareness waiting to be discovered. And discover them we must, because small irritants can become the equivalent of Chinese water torture, drip, drip, dripping on our psyches until we are worn down and worn out. Traffic is a personal torture for me. After battling noontime traffic downtown and then almost being hit by a bus a few days ago, I felt as if my teeth had been ground down a quarter of an inch. It was a good relearning, because that day, I was impatient and wanted to do my errand now, and as a result, broke my simple-solution rule of not being caught downtown during high traffic times.

By bringing your attention to the here and now and listening to your own wisdom, it's possible to come up with many simple solutions for things that aggravate you. It's overscheduled impatience that often renders us— or at least me—deaf to our own perceptions. For your own sanity, try an experiment: When an annoying situation arises, give yourself a time-out. Consciously bring your awareness into the moment. Loosen your jaw, pay attention to several breaths, and then take a deep breath and let it out with an exaggerated sigh. Sigh again…deeply and loudly. I used to cringe when my mother sighed, but I now believe she was wisely releasing excess or irritating energy.

Having relaxed a bit, smile and ask yourself, "What's a simple solution here?"

Yes, there are innumerable times when simple solutions are not enough, and there are also occasions when simplicity does bring the relief and resolution needed. Remember that no matter what the circumstances, we have the power to simplify our responses to them and our thoughts about them.

PRACTICE...

- Following are a few samples of simple solutions. You will create different ones to meet your personal needs.

Annoyance	Simple solution
Whining Child	Give five minutes of undivided attention
Being asked to do something	Say no nicely but firmly if you don't want to do it
Feeling tense	Relax your jaw, and breathe in through your nose and out through your mouth several times
Loud movie or concert	Use earplugs or headphones
Exhaustion	Take a walk or short nap
Need to vent	Talk to a trusted woman friend

THROUGHOUT YOUR DAY...

- Discover a simple solution whenever possible.

Invite serenity by trying simplicity first.

RIGHTSIZING EACH DAY

Oversized sandwiches, crammed schedules, and lives saturated with unending responsibility seem to be the trend. If you are a natural-born extrovert who thrives on lots of stimulation and nonstop doing, then perhaps you are in your element. But if you're a highly sensitive woman or simply more laid-back, trying to manage one overly stressful day after another is probably not a balanced existence for you.

A cluttered physical space and an overcrowded calendar can translate into confused thoughts and feelings. Stuff takes up space, both literally and energetically. Removing extraneous items from your physical space frees up emotional and mental room as well. Mindfulness is more likely to flourish when surrounded by inner and outer space. Becoming aware of your unique tolerance levels helps you rightsize the stuff you have and the stuff you do.

In her book Rightsizing Your Life, author Ciji Ware makes an interesting point: "People need to be mindful of what's going on in their lives now. Rightsizing is a process, not an event, and its outcome has more to do with the 'right' of the equation than the 'size.'" I resonate with the idea of rightsizing being an ongoing process, and I feel that 'right' is the operative word. What is right for you may not be right for me. Because life is the ultimate process, what is right for you at this point in time will undoubtedly change as circumstances do. For instance, if you are schooling children at home, have lots of animals to care for, or work eighty hours a week, you have much different needs than you may later. The important question is, what is the right-sized day for you now?

PRACTICE...

- Calm and quiet your body, mind, and spirit using whatever technique appeals to you now.

- From a calm center, imagine a perfectly sized day. Is such a day possible more often than not?

- If rightsizing is not an option now, how can you "better-size" your days in order to feel calmer and more balanced? For your mental and emotional welfare, please try to better-size as much as possible.

- Really see the stuff you've accumulated. Keep only what you love or need.

• Recycle, donate, or throw away something that hasn't been used in two years.

> A right-sized day has time and space for
> laughter, love, and listening.

EXPECTING THE BEST

Even if you learned to worry or expect the worst while growing up, you have the power and maturity to change those disempowering and stressful habits as an adult. Because fears and limiting expectations arise from recurrent patterns of behavior imprinted through frequent repetition, mindfulness helps you notice and alter patterns that are no longer working for you. By choosing to change a worry-prone mindset and paying attention when worry engulfs you, you have the power to transform knee-jerk responses and automatic attitudes.

As we've explored earlier, our brains are wired to focus on fearful and negative stimuli, so please don't be hard on yourself if you tend to worry and look on the dark side. But please do free yourself from the habit. There is nothing simple or serene about either worry or a fearful inclination to expect the worst. Both suck up tremendous amounts of psychic and emotional energy and waste vast quantities of time. My dad used to joke about worry by saying, "Don't tell me worrying doesn't work; most of the things I worry about never happen!" He was right. Many of the things we worry and fret about either resolve themselves or never materialize at all.

A mind preoccupied with worry and fear is unable to perceive the good, loving, and beautiful. Worry and fear block the light as surely as dark clouds block the sun. Responding to the law of magnetism, worry and fear draw more of the same toward us. Thankfully, the opposite is also true: Gratitude, calmness, and courage attract similar energies. By intentionally adopting a positive attitude, expecting the best, and replacing worry with gratitude, beneficial energy and desired outcomes will be drawn to us more often than not.

PRACTICE...

- Energy follows intention and attention. Therefore, when you become aware of worrying, set an intention to choose gratitude instead. Draw your attention to three things or people for which you feel grateful. Dwell on the reasons you are thankful for and appreciative of them.

- Express sincere, personalized gratitude to at least one person each day.

- Even if it feels contrived, imagine the best possible outcome for a stressful or hurtful situation. Embellish your fantasy outcome and enjoy it to the fullest.

- Keep practicing until you have a habit of expecting the best. Until that happens, deliberately created optimism is better than no optimism at all.

THROUGHOUT YOUR DAY...

- Choose gratitude and expect the best.

Expecting the best attracts the best;
gratitude takes care of the rest.

NOTICING SINGULAR BEAUTY

Perched atop a rock outcropping stands a single cypress tree that has become a well-known symbol of the California coastline. For over 250 years, the Lone Cypress has inspired artists, photographers, tourists, and residents who travel the 17-Mile Drive between Pacific Grove and Carmel. What is it about this one relatively small tree that makes me, and countless others, want to stay in its presence for as long as we can?

As I try to find the words to describe my response to the Lone Cypress, none seem adequate. However, my mind conjures up memories of the last time I saw the tree, and my eyes fill with tears. The Pacific Ocean was by no means passive and tranquil that day; winds howled, and huge waves surged against the Lone Cypress's rock home. Although my windbreaker was no match for the storm, I stayed put, admiring the cypress's tenacity and strength in the face of the lashing it was taking.

Perhaps I was mesmerized because the cypress stands alone, unvanquished by either the frantic wind or turbulent sea. A singular object of beauty silhouetted against the ever-changing backdrop of the vast, mysterious ocean—a symbol of survival and inspiration. Whatever the reason, I returned to our motel room drenched in awe as well as water.

It strikes me that each of us has something in common with the Lone Cypress. We are battered by storms, stand firm on rocky ground, become symbols of courage by surviving hardship with grace, and bring our own matchless beauty and inspiration to the world. Without egotism or conceit, we need to accept our own excellence. Recognizing the love, joy, compassion, and beauty you have to offer helps you accept the sacred responsibility for sharing it. As a single cypress inspired me, you can inspire others.

PRACTICE...

- Each day, be aware of one or more examples of singular beauty. Allow it to inspire you.

- Quietly pay attention to your breath as it flows naturally to and from your body.

- From a calm, centered state, invite your unique qualities of beauty and excellence to say hello. Without emotional attachment, make a list of your attributes and attitudes that can bring more light, love, and joy to people and the planet.

- Feel gratitude for these qualities.

THROUGHOUT YOUR DAY...

- Allow your singular beauty to be a blessing.

Generously share
Your beauty and excellence
Openheartedly.

Chapter 9

Fulfilling the Promise of Presence

Since life truly happens only in the here and now, presence is one of the most loving gifts you can give yourself and others.

How to fulfill the promise of presence can be

illustrated by the familiar story about a young woman who stopped a wise man on the streets of New York and asked, "Do you know the way to Carnegie Hall?" The man replied, "Practice, practice, practice."

While presence enriches our lives immeasurably, most promises of presence are not fulfilled immediately but unfold as a result of desire, intention, and, yes, practice. In this chapter, we will explore some of the many possibilities available when we are fully present to ourselves and our lives. Among them are joy, trust, wholeness, strength, love of body, and alignment with God/good.

True presence increases love and compassion. As the Buddha purportedly said, no one deserves your love and affection more than you do. Being nonjudgmentally present to yourself gives you the opportunity to fully understand, enjoy, and appreciate the unique being you are. As a result of enjoying a deep, spiritually based love and appreciation for yourself, an ever-flowing wellspring of love is created within you. From this fountainhead, compassion and caring flow freely and easily toward other beings. Because of its subsequent outflow, I believe self-love is one of the highest callings we can answer.

Simply by being attentively and openheartedly present—whether to yourself, work, family, others, or a cause—more love is added to the fabric of life, and love is the answer, no matter what the question.

AWAKENING BEGINNER'S MIND

If you've ever taken a walk with an inquisitive two-year-old or an especially olfactory-endowed dog, you know what "beginner's mind" (or, in the case of our dog, Lily, "beginner's nose") is like. Everything is worth exploring—each flower, bug, and distraction worth full attention. No matter how often Lily and I travel the same path, she is the epitome of focus and concentration on each and every smell that attracts her attention this time. Because she's absolutely present to the experience of the moment on every walk, Lily's become my guru of outdoor beginner's-mind practice.

Beginners themselves, children are great teachers of beginner's mind. A healthy child looks at the world with excitement and takes time to be truly present to all offerings. Thankfully, most young children have the luxury of enough time and energy to naturally pursue their affinity for beginner's mind. You, as a busy, responsibility-laden woman, will need to consciously create an intention toward beginner's mind and make the time to perceive with a fresh outlook.

When approached with beginner's mind, a few moments can turn into what my friend Jean called "an indelible ten minutes." Driving alone from Colorado to Iowa, Jean took a break at a rest stop in Nebraska. Instead of hurriedly eating her lunch and hopping back in the car, Jean paused to enjoy this particular view of her home state. To her surprise, she found the vista absolutely stunning.

With tears on her lashes, she told me, "I was amazed to be so moved. I even said aloud, 'This is home,' and tears rolled down my cheeks." She went on to explain, "Words can't really describe the feelings of awe and mystery that filled those ten indelible minutes of my life."

The Woman's Book of Mindfulness was written around the central theme of "a few mindful moments make a world of difference." The thought of constant mindfulness was too grandiose for me to grasp at this point in my evolution. But a few moments each day? Yes, I can do that. As each of us practices and reaps the benefits of conscious presence, I absolutely believe moments will intrinsically expand into a more mindful life.

PRACTICE...

- With openness and kind curiosity, be totally present to a person, thing, or experience at least twice a day.

- Consciously look, listen, and learn with childlike enthusiasm.

A few moments of beginner's mind can
make a world of difference.

IN-BODYING LIFE

Purposefully living in your body and paying loving and tender attention to it on a regular basis are not only helpful to your magnificent physical self, but are also some of the most effective ways to restore balance and calm to your emotions, mind, and spirit. Although it's easy to ignore our bodies and take them for granted unless they call attention to themselves by breaking down or functioning poorly, it is unwise to do so. The body is one part of the four quadrants of your being: physical, emotional, mental, and spiritual. Neglecting the body is akin to sawing one leg off a four-legged stool. Equilibrium, strength, hope, and openheartedness are achieved through respect for and attention to emotions, mind, spirit, and body.

While a few exercise programs still tout the idea of "no pain, no gain," there are innumerable programs and practices that honor body wisdom while strengthening your body. Yoga is one.

I have known Julie, a brilliant, incredibly creative, and formerly intense publisher, for over twenty years. "Brilliant" and "creative" are still excellent words to describe her, but "intense" no longer fits. What changed? She's practicing yoga. Because the practice of yoga has made such a noticeable difference in Julie's life and attitude, I asked her to share a little of her experience with you.

She writes,

> "Gentle yoga has changed my life. In only two one-and-a-half hour sessions a week, yoga enables me to completely step outside my very busy, stressful, and sometimes chaotic life to clear my mind and feel and appreciate my whole body."

For those of us who have body issues—and who among us doesn't?—Julie's next comments are especially encouraging:

"Yoga has calmed my mind and made me much more aware
and respectful of my body. I love my body now and am so
thankful it has served me well all these years."

While yoga may not be your path to living in and loving your body, please
give yourself the gift of finding some form of movement or exercise that
does help you relax and strengthen your body, soothe and transform your
emotions, calm and quiet your mind, and restore your spirit.

PRACTICE...

- Remembering that breath is the bridge between body and mind,
  gently breathe into various parts of your body—especially those that
  are uncomfortable. Thank them for all they have done and will do
  for you.

- Move. Stretch. Walk. Dance. Restore and energize your body lovingly
  and appreciatively.

THROUGHOUT YOUR DAY...

- With great respect, pay attention to your body, emotions, mind,
  and spirit.

Bridge body and soul with breath.

PERCEIVING WHOLENESS

A peach tree, plus all the fruit it will ever yield, is present in the original
seed. The same is true of us. As newborns, we are whole, brimming with
everything required for growth, learning, loving, having fun, and being
authentic. Wholeness is still within us as adults; some aspects of it are
realized while others wait their turn for potential to mature into reality.

Paradoxically, even though we have everything we need within us, it's important to remember that we're also always in some phase of beginning. Consistently uncovering yet another inner treasure—or potential challenge—is consistently the nature of evolution and growth. Being gentle and kind to the tender shoots of your beginnings, trusting the process of moving from one awareness to the next, and having patience with each step and stumble along the way are all good ways to facilitate perceiving wholeness within you. Accepting yourself as is, while compassionately aspiring to feel and express more of your inborn wholeness, is an attainable promise of presence.

Being present and truly listening to your soul's song allows you to know yourself deeply—to become acquainted with your larger spirit-self as well as the small-self each of us has acquired through trial, error, and injury. Turning within and tuning into your loving and complete spirit-self will gradually but surely instill a growing awareness of your innate wholeness and goodness into your mind and feelings.

A quiet, present mind welcomes and absorbs insights and inspiration from the Divine, whose whispers become your thoughts and in turn are reflected in your life and loves. In the sunny warmth of attention and presence, wholeness can organically reveal itself one precious realization at a time.

PRACTICE...

- After a few centering and calming breaths, breathe in the affirmation "I am whole and good." Inhale "I am..." and exhale "...whole and good."

- Invite into your mind's eye a symbol or visual image of yourself radiating wholeness.

- Rest in the certainty that wholeness is a priceless inheritance from the Divine.

- Remind yourself that you are whole, authentic, and good.

- Tap into your superb spirit-self and feel, speak, and act from her point of view.

You are simply peachy in God's eyes.

INSTILLING STRENGTH

Many fears and weaknesses hang around because we try to outrun them, ignore them, overpower them, or outthink them. This doesn't work. Banished to the sub- or unconscious minds, fears and weaknesses grow in power and potency. However, meeting our demons in the light of nonjudgmental stillness encourages them to transform into strength and empowerment.

Willingly greeting our fears and weaknesses with openness, acceptance, and respect is one of the hardest tasks mindfulness asks of us, and yet it is one of the most freeing practices we can undertake. Sitting in stillness with our sorrow and shame, our fears and judgments, laid bare is an act of courage.

The demon I'm sitting with right now is judgment of someone else, which spawns guilt and shame in me for being a "bad" woman. Only recently have I had enough self-love to really look at and accept this judgment-weakness with the goal of transforming it into strength.

As often happens when we're on a path to improved mindfulness, another perfect teacher has appeared for me. I'm feeling irritated and annoyed with a person with whom I attend a class once a week. I have a fantasy that my beloved mother, whose deathbed confession was that her main fault was being judgmental, has arranged this opportunity for me.

Mindfulness accepts experience and allows it to be our teacher. To let these experiences teach me, I am being present to my tight jaw and constricted chest whenever I see or think about a stress-inducing person. Gently, I bring my attention back to my breath and try to relax into the feelings of the moment.

Recently, I felt a glimmer of what the future might bring. Upon seeing one of my "teachers," I smiled at how creatively and speedily judgment leaped into my mind and agitated my body and emotions. Viewed with a touch of amusement, the difficult feelings dissipated quickly, which gave me

hope and helped me trust the Buddha's assurance that "Mindfulness is all-helpful."

PRACTICE...

- Sit in the stillness for a few minutes with no agenda.

- Continue sitting in the stillness. If demons surface, bless them and let them be.

- Breathe in "I am..." Breathe out "...strong and understanding."

THROUGHOUT YOUR DAY...

- Greet your feelings with gentle acceptance.

Mindfulness recognizes feelings
and experiences as teachers.

THE HEALING POWER OF LISTENING

Early in my counseling career, I realized many of my clients' yearnings could be encapsulated into three simple desires: See me. Hear me. Hold me. Undivided attention fulfills our yearning to be seen, heard, and held—held in arms or held in hearts and awareness. Attentive listening allows God to work through us. Mindfulness practice is instrumental in creating within you the unhurried calmness, emotional balance, and openheartedness it takes to truly listen.

If you've known a gifted listener, you've probably experienced coming away from their presence feeling validated, uplifted, comforted, and perhaps even blessed with a healing insight or awareness. My friend Virginia is a listener extraordinaire. Although she rarely gives advice, Virginia listens so attentively that it's not unusual for her to pinpoint exactly what is keeping the talker from feeling better, getting unstuck, or making healthier choices. Without ego—or mentioning names—she shared that she had recently had lunch with three women and each left having made a decision that had been nagging her for weeks. "After hearing their dilemmas," she explained excitedly, "it just seemed so obvious what they wanted or needed to do. I asked a question or two and they knew. It was fun."

It's also fun to listen to ourselves. Well, maybe it's not always fun, but it is essential that we listen to ourselves as completely and compassionately as we do others. How else will we know who we authentically are, what we're experiencing in the moment, and what path we'd like to take next? Listening to ourselves can be both healing and enlightening.

In his lovely book, Morning Notes, Hugh Prather wrote, "We do our best when we don't try to go it alone. Instead, we take Spirit's hand, and above all, we take Spirit's advice, which can be heard by anyone who just stops a moment and is still." Going it alone may not mean Spirit is the only one left out of the equation, we can also leave ourselves out if we don't pause to truly listen to what our hearts and minds are trying to tell us. Mindfulness helps us form loving partnerships with ourselves and Spirit.

PRACTICE...

- Quietly sit for a few moments and follow the inflow and outflow of your breath.

- Effortlessly, listen to what your mind and heart are expressing right now.

- With tenderness, hold your inner self in the ways she yearns to be held.

- Take God's hand as you return to your breath for a few more minutes.

· Lay aside any agenda you may have and truly listen either to yourself or to someone else for a few minutes.

We express love through listening.

SEEING SYNCHRONICITY

During a meditation class exercise, we went outside to mindfully notice whatever caught our eye. I was also asking for angels to be with a friend's daughter who was hovering near death. After praying, I glanced at the sky and was delighted to see a huge cloud shaped exactly as I imagine an angel wing might look. The cloud felt like an angelic nod, an assurance. My heart lifted with hope. Although she still has health challenges, my friend's daughter did survive.

At the opposite end of the spectrum, the teacher of the class noticed how the trash was spilling artistically from the trash barrel. He'd never before realized how colorful trash could be and returned to class filled with joy and gratitude that he could perceive color. I had actually observed his trash watching with a chuckle and was able to relate to what he'd seen: it was pretty. "Coincidentally," a class member whose feelings of dread about an upcoming eye surgery had kept her from noticing anything during the exercise related that our stories had turned her mind from fear toward gratitude—a pretty good miracle in itself.

Experiencing joy as a result of noticing both the ethereal and the earthy within a few mindful minutes helped me realize there must be synchronistic miracles available in every moment. We simply need to be present and awake enough to see them.

On the first anniversary of her husband's death, a friend tearfully reported she had fully awakened at 3:48 a.m., the exact minute when he had died the previous year. Since she had never awakened at that time before, she took it as a loving "wake-up call" from her husband, felt sadly joyful, and was deeply comforted by the experience.

Synchronicities, such as the angel wing cloud following my prayer and my friend's early morning visitation, make me feel heard. They deepen my belief that God, angels, loved ones, and other celestial emissaries are available and completely in love with us. The wonderful Sufi saying that tells us, "God is the Beloved who kisses us on the inside of our hearts" rings resoundingly true in the face of sweet synchronicities.

PRACTICE...

- Instead of brushing aside or barely noticing synchronicities, rest in the wonder of them.

- See synchronicities and coincidences as possible miracles, whether miniature or major.

THROUGHOUT YOUR DAY...

- Embrace the idea of being kissed on the inside of your heart by the Beloved.

It's fun to see synchronicity as
divine instant-messaging.

TRUSTING IN GOODNESS

Because trust is such a huge issue for many women, I am aware that trusting in goodness may be a hard idea to swallow. But since trust is an effective antidote for fear and insecurity, we need to trust—especially in goodness— no matter how many times we've been betrayed, wounded, or let down. Yes, there is tremendous darkness in the world, and man's inhumanity to man can break our hearts. However, we don't bring more humanity, light, and compassion into the world by concentrating on their opposites. The way to bring more good into being is to do what we can to alleviate the darkness and add light by the way we live our own lives.

An excellent way to cultivate trust in God and goodness is to recognize and act from the goodness that is within us right now, this very moment, even though we are all imperfect and are still works in progress. One of the best messages I ever received from a sermon was in the form of a little button that read PBPWMGIFWMY, an acronym for "Please Be Patient with Me, God Isn't Finished with Me Yet." No matter where you are in your evolution, without a doubt, you have more goodness in your heart than you are aware of.

To augment the ability to trust, it's important to remember that energy flows where attention goes. By focusing your awareness and attention on the goodness in and around you, positive energy flows toward it and goodness multiplies. The more goodness you become aware of and express, the easier it is to naturally trust in goodness itself. Surely seeing and creating goodness is a sacred calling.

PRACTICE...

- Sit quietly and relax into the rhythm of your breath and heartbeat.

- As you inhale, invite the soothing goodness of God to flow effortlessly into your body, mind, emotions, and spirit. As you exhale, send out goodwill and positive thoughts to whomever or whatever floats into

your awareness.

- Use the power of prayer for others. Send wishes for happiness and
peace of mind to someone.

THROUGHOUT YOUR DAY...

- Accentuate the positive by focusing on goodness.

- Consciously do one or two good deeds daily.

I inhale great draughts of space,

The east and west are mine,

and the north and south are mine.

I am larger, better than I thought,

I did not know I held so much goodness.

—Walt Whitman, "Song of the Open Road"

DOING UNTO OTHERS

Because it expresses ageless wisdom regarding living a good life, the Golden Rule is taught across the world's religions. Here are some examples:

Christianity: In everything, do unto others as you would have them do unto you.

—Jesus

Buddhism: Treat not others in ways that you yourself would find hurtful.

—Buddha

Judaism: What is hateful to you, do not do to your neighbor. This is the whole Torah; all the rest is commentary. Go and learn it.

—Hillel the Elder

Hinduism: Do not do to others what would cause pain if done to you.

—The Mahabharata

Islam: Not one of you truly believes until you wish for others what you wish for yourself.

—The Prophet Muhammad

Sufism: The basis of Sufism is consideration of the hearts and feelings of others. If you haven't the will to gladden someone's heart, then at least beware lest you hurt someone's heart, for that is our path.

—Dr. Javad Nurbakhsh

Native American Spirituality: All things are our relatives; what we do to everything, we do to ourselves.

—Black Elk, Oglala Sioux tradition

Living the Golden Rule philosophy is easier when you are present to other beings, the earth, yourself, and the moment. Conscious, aware presence to anything deepens our understanding of it. Understanding opens our hearts. Acting from the center of our hearts promotes both inner and global peace. Practiced faithfully, the Golden Rule is the only guideline we need for leading a compassionately mindful life.

PRACTICE...

- Choose your favorite version of the Golden Rule and put it in a place where you can see it often. My friend Amanda's reminder is worded humorously: "If it ain't nice, don't say it or do it!"

- Treat all beings with compassion and respect.

- Walk with gentle feet upon your Mother Earth.

THROUGHOUT YOUR DAY...

- Hold each heart, including your own, in the softest of embraces.

Do unto others...

HIGHLIGHTING LOVINGKINDNESS

Among many possible definitions for "lovingkindness" are goodwill, compassion, consideration, understanding, tender affection, and concern for the well-being of ourselves and others. Lovingkindness is a natural outcome of openheartedness, which is greatly enhanced by the practice of mindful presence.

Highlighting lovingkindness means consciously choosing to be, feel, and act kind and loving in any given moment. To help remind her to choose lovingkindness, Lenni, a client, pauses to ask herself the question, "What is loving right now in the current situation?" Lenni told me that getting the answer is not difficult but feeling loving can be tough. "Sometimes, I just say, 'yeah, right' and continue to feel anything but loving and kind. However, I've been asking the question long enough now that I rarely consciously act unloving or unkind."

Because we are human, we will not always choose lovingkindness, but since spiritual teachers and sages have taught for eons that our true nature is love, reflecting lovingkindness helps align us with our innate authenticity and our higher selves. Expressing the integrity of your highest self is one of the best ways to find peace of mind and generate a sense of joy and purpose.

Being compassionately present in the moment and consistently practicing lovingkindness allows you to bring light into shadow and comfort into sorrow. Generously sharing the priceless blessing of lovingkindness with yourself, others, and the world sends ripples of compassion and caring farther, wider, and deeper than you can ever imagine.

Light dispels darkness. Love is an attitude of light, and kindness is light in action. Therefore, fulfilling the promise of presence and performing conscious acts of lovingkindness makes us invaluable lightbearers in a time when darkness shrouds so many people and places.

May we increase light upon our precious planet by intentionally practicing lovingkindness each moment we can.

PRACTICE...

- Please remember that the practice of lovingkindness begins with self and then to others from that openhearted center.

- Spread light by being kind and loving.

- Consciously choose lovingkindness.

The gift of presence
Promises lovingkindness
Is available.

PART III

Enjoying the Benefits

Why Mindfulness Feels So Good

Mindfulness doesn't cure all, but it always cures. It corrects the mind's natural tendency toward dispersion, diffusion, and agitation, redeploying mental energy toward insight, clarity, and well-being.

—Thích Nhất Hanh

A few minutes of mindfulness can make a world of difference in how you feel and act. Mindfulness promotes awareness, understanding, nonjudgment, compassion, and peace of mind and heart.

Even if you're thrashing around in the oblivion of distraction and overwhelm, simply paying attention to your breath grounds you in the here and now, bringing you closer to balance, harmony, and awareness. As the bridge between body and mind, breath leads us home to our bodies when we've wandered far afield via such avenues as busy-ness, frustration, anxiety, or preoccupation.

Agitation and feeling overwhelmed can drop your energy levels so low that your zest for life is diminished. Practicing mindfulness is calming and centering and therefore adds to your energy storehouse. An abundance of energy enlivens you, giving you the oomph to be more engaged with yourself, others, and life in general. Mindfulness encourages energized inner and outer connections.

Along with increased energy, mindfulness promotes inner spaciousness, clarity, and well-being. While automatic behaviors and fear-driven feelings make our lives contract and cause us to hover in an atmosphere of limitation generated by our small selves, mindfully being present to our actions, reactions, and choices is incredibly expansive. In the spaciousness of expansion and peace of mind, our calm, wise, and intuitive self is able to fully function. Expansion and spaciousness open our hearts, allowing us to hear the sweet whispers of Spirit.

AWARENESS FIRST

Mindfulness leads to awareness. Awareness is the first step on the path to change. With awareness, you gain insight into the facets of your life that need balance, the parts of yourself that yearn for calm, and the times and situations in which your heart is tempted to close. With commitment, important insights can lead to equally important actions that improve your life exponentially. Bringing an intentional and nonjudgmental awareness to yourself and your environment opens your mind and heart to the best choices available. Such awareness empowers you to make wise, healthy, and mature choices based on real and appropriate needs and desires. Conscious choice is freedom.

With greater awareness of yourself, you can appreciate what is working for you and alter what isn't in gentle, supportive ways. Awareness helps you take responsibility for your personal life and become accountable for your actions and experiences. Awareness and maturity dance hand in hand. Maturity is not the over-responsible, drudgery-inducing ball and chain that perpetual Peter Pans would have us believe. Maturity is a freeing state of being that gleefully waves goodbye to any victim persona lurking within and consistently acts in ways that help create a joyful, productive, fun, and purposeful life. Awareness built through the practice of mindfulness helps us mature in loving, light, and laughter-filled ways.

One of the qualities of mindful maturity is being aware of, and making decisions based on, the greater good; what is good for us and our families as well as for our neighbors and the world in general. An example of this concept played out as I drove down the freeway this morning. About five cars ahead of me, a driver failed to notice the light had turned green. With no rude honking or hand gestures, each car behind him slowed down, giving him time to notice and move. All the drivers—including some who have probably missed a green light or two themselves—made it through the light safely. The greater good unfolded seamlessly at that intersection, and I was struck by the differences between our little vignette and the divisiveness in society and government caused by "my way is the right/only way" mentality.

Relative to your individual greater good, an incredibly important awareness to cultivate is knowing how tired you are. Tiredness dulls positive feelings and experiences and intensifies negative ones. My wonderful mother, who was often overworked and underappreciated, had a little sign in our kitchen window stating, "Dearie is Weary." As an adult, I wish I'd paid more attention to that obvious plea for a little help lightening the load. But as a kid, I simply chuckled and chalked it up as one more of Mother's endearing idiosyncrasies. If you have a similar sign hanging in a corner of your body or soul, please pay attention to it! In fact, if you get nothing more from practicing mindfulness than the awareness that you are tired and need to rest and rejuvenate, and then do so regularly, it can dramatically increase your sense of well-being and zest for life.

Although we may get a recognition chuckle from Garrison Keillor's claim that "I believe in looking reality straight in the eye and denying it," in order to really wake up to the glory of our lives, it's best if we act on Thích Nhất Hanh's belief: "Each thought, each action in the sunlight of awareness becomes sacred." Awareness is a priceless and life-enhancing benefit to be gleaned from the practice of mindfulness.

FREEDOMS THAT FOLLOW

Of course, the freedoms you gain from mindfulness will be uniquely your own, but I want to underscore a few that I know many women have come to enjoy.

Increased Authenticity

You are unique, singular, one of a kind. As Rev. Michael Beckwith asserts, "If you don't do you, then you won't be done!"

Mindful and compassionate awareness facilitates you being you. Being consistently and honestly aware of ourselves helps us understand what we authentically feel, think, desire, and have to offer. Mindfulness elicits authenticity, and authenticity invites meaning, purpose, empowerment, and joy to enhance this sacred gift of life with which we have been blessed.

We, along with our families and our world, desperately need to be able to be ourselves, to express and act from our most compassionate, wise, and strong selves…our authentic selves. When we mindfully pay attention to the trustworthy urges from our hearts and souls and give ourselves permission to live in accordance with them, we have the freedom to live authentically, and freedom itself needs our authenticity in order to thrive.

Letting Go…Letting Be…

Before I began meditating and consciously practicing mindfulness, letting go was an elusive concept to grasp. In fact, I was A+ great at grasping but not at all adept at letting go. Through increased mindfulness, I have become much better at letting go; however, I've also realized my heart doesn't resonate with that phrase. In fact, being told to "let it go" raises my hackles. To me, it sounds directive, harsh, and laden with shoulds, and my inner response is often a snappish, "Just how, exactly?" In addition, when letting go of someone or something seems impossible or takes a thousand years longer than I think reasonable, it's easy for me to drown myself in feelings of guilt and failure.

Although I totally believed in the concept of releasing and freeing ourselves from erroneous beliefs, fears, and limitations, I needed to find a different way to express it. Luckily, Paul McCartney and the Beatles provided it. In their final album, Paul wrote that his mother, Mary, who died when he was fourteen, came to him during troubled times and whispered three words of wisdom. Let it be. Ah, so…Much more gentle and flowing; I can do that. Letting challenging realities be allows me to feel successful. It helps me quit resisting what is and eventually relax into releasing attitudes, actions, expectations, and activities that constrict, rather than open, my life and heart.

Some of you may resonate with "Let it go" and some with "Let it be." To honor individual preferences, I use both throughout the book. If you have an alternate phrase that rings true to your heart, excellent.

To me, the first stanza of Reinhold Neibuhr's Serenity Prayer, as adapted by Alcoholics Anonymous, is a beautiful summation of both letting go and letting be. It is: "God, grant me the serenity to accept the things I cannot change; courage to change the things I can; and wisdom to know the difference." With mindfulness, our natural gifts for acceptance, courage, and wisdom are more easily accessible and letting be becomes possible.

Fundamentally, the best thing we can let go of is the illusion of control in this world of constant change. Yes, there are things we can change and control, but there are also many more people, events, outcomes, and viewpoints over which we have no control beyond visualizing and praying for positive resolutions. Holding on to that which we cannot control imprisons us in resistance and frustration.

Jack Kornfield, cofounder of the Insight Meditation Society, refers to the ability to let go as "the wisdom of insecurity" and explains it as, "the ability to flow with the changes, to see everything as a process of change, to relax with uncertainty." Elaborating on the idea of letting go, he says, "Meditation [and I believe we can safely add 'mindfulness'] teaches us how to let go, how to stay centered in the midst of change. Once we see that everything is impermanent and ungraspable and that we create a huge amount of suffering if we are attached to things staying the same, we realize that relaxing and letting go is a wiser way to live. Letting go does not mean not caring about things. It means caring for them in a flexible and wise way."

Please be kind to yourself as you move toward the ability to let go. While it's relatively easy to understand the wisdom of letting go, doing so is often difficult, especially with those we love the most and to whom we are strongly connected.

My neighbor, Ruth, is in the throes of letting go of many familiar patterns—self-blame and excessive worry, to name only two—as her married daughter struggles in a difficult and demeaning marriage. "One of the reasons it's so hard," Ruth says, "is that it's like watching myself all over again." After

countless sleepless nights and several heartfelt talks with her daughter, Ruth
has concluded she needs to stop believing she can control her daughter and
grandchildren's future in any way and simply love them all no matter what
happens. "For my own peace of mind, I have to stop blaming myself, put
a little distance between myself and the situation, and just love them, love
them, love them." she told me.

In order to help with the process of letting be, Ruth reminds herself she
did the best she could as a mother and young wife, pulls her thoughts
back to the moment when she drifts into fearful what-ifs, sees the beauty
and wonder in front of her right now, and is available when her daughter
and grandchildren need her. Slowly—it's especially difficult to let go when
our children are in pain—Ruth is beginning to sleep better and trust her
daughter is strong enough to handle what comes her way.

As Ruth's story illustrates, the more mindfully present we are to what is,
the less attached we become to our idea of what should be. Calmly and
nonjudgmentally paying attention to what is—even if it is painful and
difficult—keeps us from falling into what I call "the future hole of fear,"
or being locked in a prison of the past where regret and recrimination
may linger. Although it's becoming almost a cliché, the mindful awareness
received from living in the moment and staying in the here and now
continues to be a viable and valuable path to greater freedom.

Nonattachment

Nonattachment and letting be are closely connected. Being able to
incorporate both letting be and nonattachment into daily life is conducive
to emotional balance and peace of mind. In fact, the Buddha taught that the
highest happiness comes from "a mind that clings to naught."

For many years, I had the mistaken idea that it was more loving to be
absolutely attached to the outcome of all circumstances—both my own
and other people's—and I believed that feeling others' pain and confusion

almost as deeply as they did meant I really cared. I know I was taught differently during psychotherapy training, but old patterns persisted, and when I started private practice, I was still partially stuck in the same overly attached, grasping behavior with clients as I had done in my personal life. It took an illness bred of exhaustion and an overactive sense of responsibility to show me that my attachment had landed me in the same emotional pit my clients inhabited.

Nonattachment does not mean disconnectedness or indifference. When we're able to be compassionately nonattached, we actually feel more engaged with and connected to ourselves and other people. Letting go of attachment, especially attachment to a specific outcome, minimizes resistance to our own struggles; it also frees us from the persistent belief that we must somehow "make it all better" for everyone else, no matter what their challenge. Very tiring! But no matter how exhausting this idea can be, it's disturbingly common for women to believe at a deep level that everything is our fault, and therefore, fixing it—whatever "it" may be—is our responsibility.

Letting go of that exhausting belief and accepting the fact that others are responsible for themselves and their lives gives us the energy and desire to be mindfully present for them in caring and compassionate ways.

As a variation of Jack Kornfield's "wisdom of insecurity," my husband Gene likes to use the phrase "wisdom of impermanence." One of the wonderful benefits of mindfulness is that it helps us realize the reality of impermanence and trust its ultimate wisdom, even when we don't have a clue what that wisdom will turn out to be. The greatest lessons I ever learned about the pain, grace, and wisdom of impermanence came from working with hospice. The intensity and immediacy of death, dying, and grief elicit a mindful presence. As a facilitator for grief support groups, I was awed by the courage and grace with which people dealt with loss and change. Being privy to some of the ways people rose from the ashes of grief and recreated different but nonetheless rewarding lives after the death of a spouse, child, parent, or friend gave me an abiding trust in the resilience of the human spirit. Visiting with hospice patients and their caretakers, as both a therapist and chaplain taught me invaluable and enduring lessons about the art and joy of impermanence, letting go, letting be, and nonattachment. Not without many tears, of course, but tears are an integral part of the blessed whole of life.

Lightening Up

Feeling lighter comes naturally as a result of letting go and developing compassionate nonattachment for situations over which you have no responsibility or control. Lightening up also comes when you quiet your mind and establish positive and upbeat thinking habits. Although sometimes used harshly and inappropriately, the expression "Lighten up" is wise advice—advice that most of us need and all of us are capable of bringing to fruition.

As we turn our attention to lightening up, mindfulness is an essential practice. It helps bring awareness and healing to inner wounds and limiting beliefs that darken our attitudes and deplete our positive attributes. Being compassionately present to yourself deepens your understanding of who you really are and opens your heart and mind to the wisdom, beauty, and goodness that reside at the core of your being. Mindfulness helps you live as American Indian sage White Eagle suggests: "Be still within, be calm. Do not try to overdrive your life. Do your work quietly; live as the flowers live, opening your heart to the sunlight of God's love."

Basking in the glow of divine grace and self-love lights the fire of compassion in your heart and lightens up every aspect of your being, doing, feeling, and believing. The practice of mindfulness illumines the path to joy and well-being.

WALKING MINDFULLY

The real wonder, as Vietnamese monk Thích Nhất Hanh has said, is not to walk on water, but to walk mindfully on this green earth.

- Breath guides you home.

- Mindfulness leads to a quiet mind and an open heart.

- Compassionate inner awareness encourages self-love and acceptance.

- Lovingkindness toward yourself fills you to overflowing, enabling you to love others more fully and freely.

- Mindfully focusing attention on the current moment helps restore balance, harmony, and hope.

- Simplicity facilitates serenity.

- Control is illusion, change is inevitable, impermanence is immutable. Engage completely with the reality of now.

- Mindfulness helps you remember you are a remarkable, powerful, and compassionate woman.

- Live gently with yourself and others.

May you be mindful. May each step taken upon this beautiful green earth be blessed with compassionate awareness, gentle acceptance, and peace of mind and heart.

A few mindful moments
can make a world of difference.

———————————————

Chapter 10 | Why Mindfulness Feels So Good

Acknowledgments

Writing The Woman's Book of Mindfulness was originally a grace-filled endeavor in which everything fell into place, inspiration flowed, I learned a lot while enjoying the process, and—amazingly—the computer even behaved. True to form, updating and refreshing The Woman's Book of Mindfulness for its new incarnation has been a hope-giving and heart-lifting experience. It has been a huge joy reuniting with the inimitable Brenda Knight. Brenda's magical wisdom and creative brilliance have lighted many paths throughout my writing career, and it makes my heart sing with gratitude to be working with her again. In fact, everyone I've had the good fortune to interact with at Books That Save Lives has been great: friendly, creative, patient, inspiring, professional, and fun! A big thank you to Debbie Hartung, who promptly answered all my questions and requests with cheerful acumen. Were it not for Robin Miller's written instructions and kindly-delivered tutoring, I would have been lost in an abyss of formatting ferment. With her help, the style guide stuff turned out to be fun. The cover is beautiful, Jermaine Lau! You exemplified Books That Save Live's philosophy of partnership with its authors by graciously inviting me to share my cover ideas and desires with you. I loved the process and the result. Thank you…

As always, gobs of gratitude to my kindhearted, supportive, and adventurous husband, Gene, without whom I would never have published a word.

References

Aron, Elaine. 1998. *The Highly Sensitive Person: How to Survive When the World Overwhelms You*. New York: Broadway Books.

Baraz, James. 2007. Awakening Joy (online course). www.awakeningjoy.info.

Bowen, Will. 2007. *A Complaint Free World: How to Stop Complaining and Start Enjoying the Life You've Always Wanted*. New York: Doubleday.

Buechner, Frederick. 1999. *The Eyes of the Heart: A Memoir of the Lost and Found*. New York: Harper Collins.

Chodron, Pema. 2001. *Start Where You Are: A Guide to Compassionate Living*. Boston: Shambhala Classics.

Cooke, Grace. 1972. *The Quiet Mind*. Hampshire, England: The White Eagle Publishing Trust.

Gammons, Peter. 2007. "What I learned." *USA Today*, March 7.

Lucado, Max. 2006. *Cure for the Common Life: Living in Your Sweet Spot*. Houston: Thomas Nelson.

Prather, Hugh. 2005. *Morning Notes: 365 Meditations to Wake You Up*. Berkeley, CA: Conari Press.

Siegel, Bernie. 1986. *Love, Medicine, and Miracles*. New York: Harper and Row.

Thoele, Sue Patton. 2001. *The Courage to Be Yourself: A Woman's Guide to Emotional Strength and Self-Esteem*. Berkeley, CA: Conari Press.

_____. 1996. *Heart Centered Marriage: Fulfilling Our Natural Desire for Sacred Partnership*. Berkeley, CA: Conari Press.

Ware, Ciji. 2007. *Rightsizing Your Life: Simplifying Your Surroundings While Keeping What Matters Most*. New York: Springboard Press.

Photo Credits: Brett Hall

Author Biography

Sue Patton Thoele is the author of numerous books including The Courage to Be Yourself, Strength: Meditations for Wisdom, Balance, & Power, The Courage to Be a Stepmom, and The Woman's Book of Courage. She is a mom, stepmom, grandmother, wife, and retired psychotherapist and women's group leader. Sue loves playing with words, swimming with wild dolphins, being creative, and hanging out with friends and family, both two-footed and four-footed.

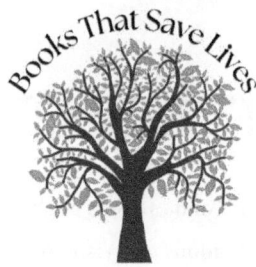

Books That Save Lives came into being in 2024 when the editor and publisher, Brenda Knight, heard directly from readers and authors that certain self-help, grief, psychology books, and journals were providing a lifeline for folks. We live in a stressful world where it is increasingly difficult not to feel overwhelmed, worried, depressed, and downright scared. We intend to offer support for the vulnerable, including people struggling with mental wellness and physical illness as well as people of color, queer and trans adults and teens, immigrants and anyone who needs encouragement and inspiration.

From first responders, military veterans, and retirees to LGBTQ+ teens and to those experiencing the shock of bereavement and loss, our books have saved lives. To us, there is no higher calling.

We would love to hear from you! Our readers are our most important resource; we value your input, suggestions, and ideas.

Please stay in touch with us and follow us at:

www.booksthatsavelives.net

https://www.instagram.com/booksthatsavelives/

www.ingramcontent.com/pod-product-compliance
Lightning Source LLC
Chambersburg PA
CBHW021142090426
42740CB00008B/897